STERLING BIOGRAPHIES

JIM THORPE

An Athlete for the Ages

Ellen C. Labrecque

STERLING

New York / London
www.sterlingpublishing.com/kids

For Jeff

STERLING and the distinctive Sterling logo are registered trademarks of
Sterling Publishing Co., Inc.

Library of Congress Cataloging-in-Publication Data
Labrecque, Ellen.
Jim Thorpe : an athlete for the ages / by Ellen Labrecque.
    p. cm. — (Sterling biographies)
Includes bibliographical references and index.
ISBN 978-1-4027-6365-6 (pbk.) — ISBN 978-1-4027-7150-7 (hardcover)
1. Thorpe, Jim, 1887–1953—Juvenile literature. 2. Athletes—United States—
Biography—Juvenile literature. 3. Indian athletes—United States—Biography—
Juvenile literature. I. Title.
  GV697.T5L33 2010
  796.092—dc22
  [B]
                                                                        2009024231

Lot #: 10 9 8 7 6 5 4 3 2 1
12/09

Published by Sterling Publishing Co., Inc.
387 Park Avenue South, New York, NY 10016
© 2010 by Ellen C. Labrecque

Distributed in Canada by Sterling Publishing
c/o Canadian Manda Group, 165 Dufferin Street
Toronto, Ontario, Canada M6K 3H6
Distributed in the United Kingdom by GMC Distribution Services
Castle Place, 166 High Street, Lewes, East Sussex, England BN7 1XU
Distributed in Australia by Capricorn Link (Australia) Pty. Ltd.
P.O. Box 704, Windsor, NSW 2756, Australia

Printed in China
All rights reserved

Sterling ISBN 978-1-4027-7150-7 (hardcover)
         ISBN 978-1-4027-6365-6 (paperback)

Image research by Jim Gigliotti and James Buckley, Jr.

For information about custom editions, special sales, premium and corporate
purchases, please contact Sterling Special Sales Department at 800-805-5489
or specialsales@sterlingpublishing.com.

Contents

Events in the Life of Jim Thorpe

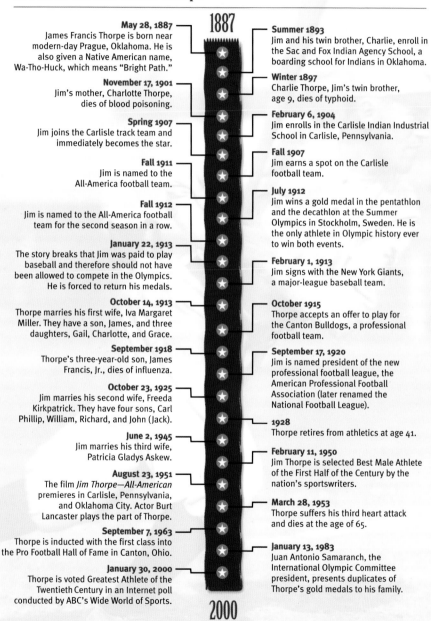

1887

May 28, 1887
James Francis Thorpe is born near modern-day Prague, Oklahoma. He is also given a Native American name, Wa-Tho-Huck, which means "Bright Path."

November 17, 1901
Jim's mother, Charlotte Thorpe, dies of blood poisoning.

Spring 1907
Jim joins the Carlisle track team and immediately becomes the star.

Fall 1911
Jim is named to the All-America football team.

Fall 1912
Jim is named to the All-America football team for the second season in a row.

January 22, 1913
The story breaks that Jim was paid to play baseball and therefore should not have been allowed to compete in the Olympics. He is forced to return his medals.

October 14, 1913
Thorpe marries his first wife, Iva Margaret Miller. They have a son, James, and three daughters, Gail, Charlotte, and Grace.

September 1918
Thorpe's three-year-old son, James Francis, Jr., dies of influenza.

October 23, 1925
Jim marries his second wife, Freeda Kirkpatrick. They have four sons, Carl Phillip, William, Richard, and John (Jack).

June 2, 1945
Jim marries his third wife, Patricia Gladys Askew.

August 23, 1951
The film *Jim Thorpe—All-American* premieres in Carlisle, Pennsylvania, and Oklahoma City. Actor Burt Lancaster plays the part of Thorpe.

September 7, 1963
Thorpe is inducted with the first class into the Pro Football Hall of Fame in Canton, Ohio.

January 30, 2000
Thorpe is voted Greatest Athlete of the Twentieth Century in an Internet poll conducted by ABC's Wide World of Sports.

Summer 1893
Jim and his twin brother, Charlie, enroll in the Sac and Fox Indian Agency School, a boarding school for Indians in Oklahoma.

Winter 1897
Charlie Thorpe, Jim's twin brother, age 9, dies of typhoid.

February 6, 1904
Jim enrolls in the Carlisle Indian Industrial School in Carlisle, Pennsylvania.

Fall 1907
Jim earns a spot on the Carlisle football team.

July 1912
Jim wins a gold medal in the pentathlon and the decathlon at the Summer Olympics in Stockholm, Sweden. He is the only athlete in Olympic history ever to win both events.

February 1, 1913
Jim signs with the New York Giants, a major-league baseball team.

October 1915
Thorpe accepts an offer to play for the Canton Bulldogs, a professional football team.

September 17, 1920
Jim is named president of the new professional football league, the American Professional Football Association (later renamed the National Football League).

1928
Thorpe retires from athletics at age 41.

February 11, 1950
Jim Thorpe is selected Best Male Athlete of the First Half of the Century by the nation's sportswriters.

March 28, 1953
Thorpe suffers his third heart attack and dies at the age of 65.

January 13, 1983
Juan Antonio Samaranch, the International Olympic Committee president, presents duplicates of Thorpe's gold medals to his family.

2000

Simply the Best

That was the proudest moment of my life.

It was a clear day in Stockholm, Sweden, on July 15, 1912—the last day of the fifth Olympic Games. Sweden's King Gustav V stood at a podium in the middle of the Olympic stadium. The king handed out medals to the winning athletes.

Soon it was time for one particular American athlete, James Francis Thorpe, to receive his medal. When Thorpe walked to the podium, the crowd in the stadium came alive. The king handed Thorpe his first gold medal, this one for winning the **pentathlon**. Moments later, it was Thorpe's turn to walk to the podium again. This gold medal was for the last event of the Games, the **decathlon**. The king placed the second medal around Thorpe's neck. Then the Swedish leader, who came from a long line of royalty, spoke in awe to the Native American, who came from such humble beginnings: "Sir, you are the greatest athlete in the world," the king told Thorpe. Thorpe had the courage only to mumble back, "Thanks, King."

Later, Thorpe described this exchange with the king as "the proudest moment of [his] life." And, he was indeed the greatest athlete in the world. But Thorpe's life, within as well as outside of athletics, was also filled with great heartache and despair. Jim Thorpe was a simple man, but his life, and the times in which he lived, were often complicated.

CHAPTER 1

Young Jim

Our lives were lived out in the open, winter and summer. We were never in the house when we could be out of it.

Early in the morning of May 28, 1887, the sun was shining brightly outside the home of Charlotte Thorpe. Thorpe, a Native American of Potawatomi and Kickapoo descent, had just given birth to twin baby boys, James Francis and Charles, in a one-room cabin with a dirt floor. Shortly after her sons' birth, Charlotte thought about what Indian names she should call them.

Jim Thorpe was part Sac and Fox Indian. Keokuk, who is shown in this painting from 1837, was a famous Sac and Fox chief who cooperated with the United States government in land disputes.

Indian versus Native American

Upon arriving at the Americas, the explorer Christopher Columbus mistakenly believed he had reached the Indies. He named the native people he found in North and South America "Indians." This misnomer has continued to be in use for much of American history. Today, some native people prefer the label "Native Americans," while others prefer "American Indians." But in Jim Thorpe's time, he and his people called themselves Indians.

In addition to "official" English names, it was customary in Native American culture for a mother to give her child an Indian name with special significance. Charlotte lay in bed holding one of her boys, James, and stared out her bedroom window. Soon, she noticed a trail dazzling beneath the sunshine. Charlotte immediately knew the Indian name she would call James: Wa-Tho-Huck, which means "Bright Path." She simply had a feeling this son would do some great things in his life.

James, or Jim, Thorpe and his twin brother, Charles, or Charlie, were born to Hiram P. Thorpe, who was half Sac and Fox Indian and half Irish, and their mother, Charlotte, who was almost all Native American, and just a quarter French. Hiram was muscular and athletic and known as one of the strongest men in the land. He could walk thirty miles a day while hunting and barely get tired. Charlotte was a devoted and loving mother and

She simply had a feeling this son would do some great things in his life.

Shameful Treatment

The treatment of Indians during the nineteenth century is one of the most shameful atrocities of United States history. In 1830, President Andrew Jackson signed the Indian Removal Act, which encouraged Native Americans in the East to move west of the Mississippi River. This way, the white men could take over and develop their domain.

Most Indians did not leave peacefully. They had already been there for years before the white men arrived. They did not believe in the concept of owning land.

Tribes fought against the U.S. military for years, and thousands of lives—those of both Indians and whites—were lost. Many Indians also died when they were forced to march across the country. During one march in 1838, now called "the Trail of Tears," 4,000 Indians died from the cold, disease, and starvation.

In the late 1800s, Native Americans still resisted the migration. And the Indians who had already been forced out West were still considered second class. They lived without the basic rights of white men who were U.S. citizens, such as voting privileges and the right to own land, and many were not permitted to leave their reservations. As a result, many Indians, including Jim's father, Hiram, felt bitterness and anger against the government. Jim and his brother, Charlie, were born under this cloud of violence and discontent.

Andrew Jackson, who signed the Indian Removal Act, was the seventh president of the United States. He held the office from 1829 to 1837.

wife. It is believed that Hiram and Charlotte met at a **powwow**, or large Indian gathering. At the time of their meeting, Hiram already had two other wives and three children. Back in those days, **polygamy** was an accepted practice in Indian culture. In addition to Jim and Charlie, Charlotte and Hiram had nine other children together. Five of those nine died in infancy or early childhood. Life on the frontier was harsh, and diseases spread quickly.

The Thorpes lived along the North Canadian River in present-day Oklahoma. (Oklahoma did not become a state until 1907.) Their home was first considered part of a reservation, or a piece of land set aside by the U.S. government for Native Americans. But in 1887, the year Jim and Charlie were born, the government passed the General Allotment Act. Through this act, the government divided up reservation land and parceled it among Indian families. Each person in a family was given 160 acres. In the Thorpe family, this worked out to about 1,200 acres along the river on which to live, farm, and raise livestock.

Although the Thorpes were by no means rich, Hiram kept his family well fed and sheltered. He planted a variety of crops such as corn, beans, and squash, and also raised horses, cattle, hogs, and chickens. Charlotte was in charge of the crops, while Hiram tended to the animals.

"We always had plenty to eat at our house," Jim said about his early days. The fact that food was in abundance was important: after all, Jim spent his entire childhood running and playing—and he needed energy!

Growing Up Outside

Jim and Charlie were inseparable in early childhood. The boys were not identical twins: Jim had his father's strong jaw and black hair, while Charlie had a darker complexion and brown hair. But the boys' interests were surely the same. The twins spent their days exploring the woodland around their family's home. They fished and swam in the river, or searched the forest for blackberries and grapes to eat. As young as age six, they also hunted small animals, such as squirrels and rabbits, with bows and arrows and small rifles. One of Jim's favorite meals made from their catches was fried squirrel with gravy and biscuits. "Our lives were lived out in the open, winter and summer," Jim said about this early time in his life. "We were never in the house when we could be out of it."

Although the brothers were the best of friends, they were also competitive. They loved to wrestle and have running and swimming races. Even at this early age, it was clear how naturally athletic Jim was. He usually ran faster, jumped higher, and was a better marksman than Charlie. One of the boys' favorite games was follow-the-leader. The leader did things like swim in rivers, climb trees, and even run under horses! "Our sports were not ordered or directed," Jim said about this time. "But, they did lay the foundation for future big performances."

Strict School Days

As much as Jim's mother and father encouraged outdoor play, they still wanted their children to attend school. Hiram and Charlotte were two of the few people in the area who could read and write, both having attended Kansas schools in their youth. They wanted the same for their own children. When the boys were six, in 1893, Hiram enrolled them at the Sac and Fox Indian Agency School, which was more than twenty miles from their home. A religious group called the Quakers founded the school in 1872, and it was meant for children with any Sac and Fox heritage. Students ranged in age from five to twenty. In addition to attending classes, students were also expected to live at the school. The mission there was to teach the students how to read and write as well as to teach them job skills, such as how to use farm tools. At the time, Indians and the Indian way of life were considered inferior to white people and their culture. The Indian students had to cut their long hair, were made to wear heavy wool suits instead of the freer Indian attire, and were forced to speak English, as opposed to their tribe's native language. The students also had to follow a strict schedule. A ringing bell told them it was time to wake up, switch classes, or attend a meal. Disobeying any of the rules resulted in a spanking by a teacher. "Our lives were just one bell after another," one student recalled. "Everything was routine work and much different than our free life on the reservation."

> *The Indian students had to cut their long hair, were made to wear heavy wool suits . . . and were forced to speak English.*

Charlie, who was more easygoing than Jim, adapted fairly well to this strict routine. Jim, on the other hand, could not stand school. He struggled with being inside so much and having to sit still all the time. He missed the free-roaming, outside life he had enjoyed back home. As a result, Jim ran away from school many times, using the North Canadian River to guide him. When he arrived home, his father yelled at him, sometimes hit him, then put him in his wagon and took him back to the school. Jim wasn't the only student to run away at this time. In 1896, the superintendent even requested military troops to help round up all the runaway students.

After Jim repeatedly ran away from the Sac and Fox School, his father placed him in the Haskell Institute (pictured here) in Lawrence, Kansas.

In early 1897, life changed for the worse at the Sac and Fox School. A typhoid epidemic, or widespread disease, swept through the school. Many students became extremely sick, including Charlie. Despite care and attention from his teachers, Charlie died in the spring at the age of nine.

Jim was devastated to lose his brother and best friend. Without Charlie, school became even more unbearable. Jim ran away from the Sac and Fox School again the following spring. His father once again took him back to school in his wagon. But according to lore, by the time Hiram had returned home, Jim had already run away from school, taken a shortcut, and beaten Hiram to their door! Hiram became determined to find a new school for his son that was far enough away that Jim could not escape. He found this school in Lawrence, Kansas, at the Haskell Institute—nearly three hundred miles from Jim's cabin in Oklahoma.

Learning to Love Sports

Jim traveled to Haskell on a train in the fall of 1898. Just eleven years old at the time, Jim was overwhelmed by

the sprawling Haskell campus and by the giant, gray, stone buildings. Soon enough, though, routine at the Haskell Institute proved to be similar to the one at the Sac and Fox School. Like Sac and Fox, the Haskell Institute was a school just for Native Americans. Haskell, though, had more students than Sac and Fox—the students came from ninety different tribes. Days were still dictated by bells from dawn to dusk, and the students had to wear military-type uniforms. They spent four hours a day in the classroom, while another four hours were spent learning a trade, such as house painting or baking. Once again, Jim struggled with the strict discipline the school administrators enforced.

It was during his Haskell days that Jim's love of athletics blossomed. Instead of the freewheeling recreation of his youth, Jim discovered at Haskell a more organized version of athletics. Haskell had a strong sports program that competed against other schools and even some colleges. Thorpe was too young to play on the **varsity** squads, but he spent many hours hanging around the practices of the football, baseball, and track teams, watching the athletes.

In 1901, about three years after Jim arrived at Haskell, he received an urgent letter from home. His father had been shot in the chest in a hunting accident. Panicked that he would lose his dad, Jim jogged down to the railroad station in Lawrence and sneaked onto an empty boxcar. About 100 miles into the ride, Jim discovered the train was heading away from his home in Oklahoma— not toward it. He hopped off the train and started following the tracks back. It took about two weeks of hopping trains, bumming wagon rides, and simply walking, but Jim made it home.

Thorpe was too young to play on the varsity squads, but he spent many hours hanging around the practices of the football, baseball, and track teams, watching the athletes.

When Jim arrived at his cabin, he discovered his father had already recovered from his hunting accident. Hiram was furious at his son for once again running away from school without permission. He beat Jim as punishment and tried to force him back to school, but this time Jim refused. Hiram realized he wasn't going to win this battle with his stubborn son. Jim was not going back to Haskell.

For the next couple months, Jim helped his father on the farm. Life on the Canadian River was going along well, until Jim's mother passed away from blood poisoning on November 17, 1901. Just as when Charlie died, Jim was devastated. He withdrew from the people around him and began to help less with work on the farm. One day, after Jim and his older brother George went fishing instead of watching over the livestock, Jim's father was irate. Instead of waiting around for Hiram to beat him again, Jim ran—this time away from home,

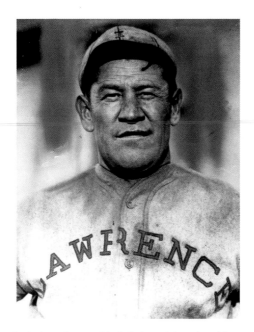

An older Jim, who is shown in an undated photograph here, loved the sports programs at the Lawrence, Kansas, school. But after he ran away from the Haskell Institute, he refused to go back.

not toward it. He headed toward the Texas border, where he heard he could find work on one of the many growing ranches. At age thirteen, Jim ended up on a ranch in Texas, mending fences and taming wild horses.

Soon Jim earned enough money to buy a team of horses himself. He arrived back at his front door and presented the horses to his father as a peace offering. Hiram accepted the horses and allowed his son to live at home again—but only if Jim attended the Garden Grove School, a public school that was intended for Indians as well as white children. The school was just a mile away from their home. Relieved that he didn't have to attend a boarding school again, Jim accepted the conditions.

CHAPTER 2

Welcome to Carlisle

I believe in immersing Indians in our civilization, and when we get them under, holding them there until they are thoroughly soaked.

—Lieutenant Richard Henry Pratt

In early 1904, a guest speaker arrived in Jim's classroom at Garden Grove. The man was from Carlisle Indian Industrial School—the country's first and largest government-funded Indian school. He told the students about life at Carlisle and about the trades they could learn. Jim's ears perked up, though, when the speaker talked of Carlisle's sports programs. Carlisle's football team competed against some of the nation's best colleges—and won.

Although Jim had yet to play on any teams that competed against other schools, he loved athletics of all kinds. A teacher at Garden Grove, Walter White, organized track meets for his students. Thorpe could jump higher than any other kid at the school—even older boys. During pickup baseball games, Jim could throw harder and hit the ball farther than any of the other students. Locals who came to watch the games talked about "that young Indian" who was a star on the field.

Around this time, Jim was also ready for a change in his life. His father's cabin was more crowded than ever. Hiram had remarried after Charlotte passed away. He and his new wife were starting another family together.

In this photo, students at the Carlisle School in the early 1900s participate in a physical-education class.

Hiram also thought it was time for Jim to move on. Soon after the recruiter spoke at Garden Grove, Jim's dad wrote a letter to the local Sac and Fox Agency. "I have a boy that I Wish you could Make rangements to Send of to School," the letter stated. "I want him to go and make something of him Self."

Despite the poor grammar by today's standards, Hiram's letter worked. The agency agreed to send Jim to Carlisle and pay his transportation and school costs. Jim, age sixteen, enrolled in the Carlisle Indian School. Before Jim left home, his father said goodbye with these final words: "Son, you are an Indian. I want you to show other races what an Indian can do."

Back to Boarding School

The Carlisle Indian School was founded by Lieutenant Richard Henry Pratt of the United States Army. It opened on

Shown above is Jim's student information card from his days at Carlisle Indian Industrial School.

November 1, 1879. Located on the northern edge of the town of Carlisle, Pennsylvania, the school was in the thick of coal country. The campus was on twenty-seven acres of well-kept green lawns with a white picket fence encircling the land.

Like the other Indian boarding schools Jim had attended, this one was run in a militaristic style. Students were up at 5:30 a.m. Their mornings were filled with academic classes, and their afternoons consisted of work training such as tailoring, shoemaking, and carpentry. The students were expected to study four hours a night. "We keep them moving," Pratt explained about life for the students. "They have no time for homesickness—none for mischief—none for regret."

The academic level at Carlisle equaled that of a regular high school, but students' ages ranged from ten to twenty-seven years. The course of study was fierce. Students were expected to sign up for two five-year terms. As a result, Carlisle had few graduates. Of the 8,000 students who attended the school from 1879 to when it closed in 1918, only 761 earned a diploma.

In addition to the intense academic curriculum, Carlisle stood out from other Indian boarding schools for another reason: its top-notch sports program. Pratt believed in the importance of athletics. "Strong minds and weak bodies will not do," Pratt said.

The lieutenant urged his students to fish and camp in the surrounding woods. He also suggested starting a cycling club. Most of the students' favorite athletic pursuit, though, was football. The physical-activity teacher, W. G. Thompson, introduced the game to his pupils, and they were hooked immediately. For the first years, the game was played just between Carlisle students—and more for fun than anything else. But in the fall of 1894, Carlisle played its first intercollegiate schedule against schools such as Dickinson College, the U.S. Naval Academy (Navy), and Bucknell University. (Although Carlisle was like a high school in terms of academics, it played against colleges in athletics.) Carlisle did not win any games against the colleges, but it did earn the respect of the other schools, as well as the fans. The team had "outstanding speed and potential," one newspaper writer stated.

Most of the students' favorite athletic pursuit, though, was football.

When Jim arrived on campus in 1904, the Indians, as all the school's teams were known, had become a football powerhouse. In the fall of 1903, Carlisle had its best season in school history. It finished with a record of 11–2–1 (11 wins, 2 losses, and 1 tie), and its **quarterback**, Jimmie Johnson, was named an **All-America**, one of college sports' top honors. Jim, on the other hand, appeared to be better suited to be the team's water

Pratt's Belief

Richard Henry Pratt, the founder of the Carlisle Indian Industrial School, believed that Native Americans could be as smart and as civilized as white people—they just had to be educated. At this time, the Indians' way of life was very different from white ways. Because their lifestyle was so different, white people viewed Indians as less human than themselves.

Pratt came to his belief in 1875 as a military commander in Indian Territory. Pratt's job was to keep Indian tribes on their reservations and away from white settlers. The Indians, who resented this supervision, attacked the settlers in search of food and buffalo meat and skins. Pratt was told to lock up Indian chiefs in chains and put them in prison until the raids stopped. While guarding these prisoners, Pratt started to feel sorry for treating Indians so poorly. He thought it would be better to teach the Indians to live like white people, rather than imprison them. He let them out of their chains, and allowed them to walk freely. He cut their hair, gave them Western clothing, and began to educate them.

Richard Henry Pratt was a former military man who founded the Carlisle Indian Industrial School.

When the Indians were finally set free after three years in captivity, Pratt felt his job to help the Indian race had just begun. (Today, of course, that view would be seen as controversial, but it was considered a good plan in those days.) Pratt started the Carlisle School a year later. His vision for the school never changed in the twenty-five years he was in charge. He wanted to help Native Americans become "equal" to whites by teaching them to adopt white culture.

Young Jim (standing) is pictured here with friends.

boy than the football star he would become in later years. At sixteen, Thorpe stood just 5 feet 5 inches and weighed a mere 115 pounds. Although he would have loved to join the varsity football team right away, he was simply too small.

Thorpe focused his first couple of months at Carlisle on adjusting to his new, regimented routine. He was just getting settled when he received devastating news from home. His father, Hiram, had died from a snakebite on April 24. Hiram had been fifty-two years old. Jim was beside himself with grief. After his father's death, he slipped into depression. To help their student through his grief, teachers thought it would be a good time for Thorpe to participate in the school's "outing" program. The program, designed by Lieutenant Pratt in 1880, sent Carlisle students off campus to live with white families in a work-study environment. Jim left campus on June 17, 1904, just four months after he had arrived.

Taking a Break

The idea behind the outing program was to help Indians improve their English as well as learn more about white culture. Students stayed with a family for three months, or sometimes longer.

Jim's first experience in this program was on a farm in Somerton, Pennsylvania. His days were spent inside the family's house, mopping floors, peeling potatoes, and boiling laundry. Jim earned just five dollars a month; the average monthly salary for white Americans at this time was thirty-three dollars a month.

Carlisle youngsters learned skills that school officials felt would help them adapt to white culture. These boys are making (or repairing) shoes.

The boy who loved the outdoors couldn't stand the inside work. He decided to do what he always did when he was unhappy: he ran away. This time, instead of running away from a school, Jim ran back to Carlisle. He hadn't been back long when he was sent on another outing—this one to a farm in Dolington, Pennsylvania. After a brief stint working in its garden, Jim was moved to another farm in Robbinsville, New Jersey. There he was put in charge of a team of Indian workers, where they planted row upon row of vegetables. Jim resented the low pay (he only made eight dollars a month) and felt like a servant—not like a part of anybody's family as promised by the school.

In April 1907, he'd had enough of his situation once again. Running through forests and hitching rides on wagons, Jim arrived back on campus. This time, instead of the administrators sending him to another farm, they let him stay. He was still severely punished for disobedience. Thorpe was put in a cell for four days in a dark, windowless basement. Relieved to be away from the farm, Jim did not complain. When he was released from the dank cell, he was happy. Perhaps he felt the big changes that were in store for him. Just shy of twenty, Jim was on the brink of athletic stardom. The world would soon meet its greatest athlete.

CHAPTER 3

The Natural

Nobody is going to tackle Jim!

In the spring of 1907, Jim walked across the Carlisle campus. His solitary confinement behind him, he moved as easily as the wind. Thorpe was on his way to play in a football game with friends—his favorite afternoon activity. The nineteen-year-old had grown—he now stood 5 feet 11 inches and weighed 160 pounds of mostly muscle. As Jim strolled under the bright sunshine, he noticed some varsity track athletes practicing the high jump. He stopped a minute to watch. After each jumper cleared the bar, they raised it to another level. When the bar was raised to 5 feet 9 inches, none of the athletes could make it over this height. Jim, dressed in overalls and borrowed gym shoes, sauntered over and asked: "Could I give it a try?" The guys told Jim to give it his best shot, expecting to get a good chuckle over his performance.

Jim raced toward the pit, lifted off the ground, twisted his body, arched his back, and sailed over the bar with ease. He landed softly in the sandpit. The young man stood up, brushed himself off, then raced off toward the football game. The high jumpers looked at each other in disbelief. This unknown student had just broken the school's high-jump record—wearing overalls!

The next day, one of the high jumpers, Harry Archenbald, walked into his coach's office to tell him what had happened. Pop Warner, who was the track coach as

Jim was a track star at Carlisle. He was a natural athlete who excelled at any sport he tried.

well as the head football coach, immediately called for Thorpe.

When Thorpe arrived at Warner's office, Pop put his arm around Jim's broad shoulders. He told the young man to go get a track uniform, because as of that afternoon, Thorpe was officially a member of the varsity team.

Carlisle's Football Tradition

Jim's first season on the track team was a smashing success. He won the high jump and high hurdles at the Carlisle School games. He also finished second in the high hurdles and high jump against Bucknell University. Thorpe broke most of his school's track and field records.

"Before Jim hit Carlisle, I was quite the athlete around here," teammate Albert Exendine remembered. "I held the records in the long jump and the high jump, the shot put, and the hammer, and several other track-and-field events. But it took Jim just one day to break all my records."

Once track season finished, Jim still yearned to play team sports—specifically, he wanted to earn a varsity spot on the legendary Carlisle football team.

In 1907, the Carlisle Indians were one of the best, if not the best, college football teams in the nation. The program had started five years after the school was established. In the early seasons, the team drew crowds because fans wanted to see what Indians looked like playing the "American" game. One fan was actually disappointed by how normal the players looked. "Oh, dear me," she proclaimed. "Are those the Indians? Why, they don't look any different from our boys."

"Oh, dear me," she proclaimed. "Are those the Indians? Why, they don't look any different from our boys."

As the Indians became more skilled at the game, other teams stopped thinking of them as a **novelty** act. Instead, they started seeing them as a fearsome opponent. The better Carlisle became, the more they had to contend with unfair officiating. Some referees did not like seeing the Indians beat the traditional football powerhouses. They tried to stop them from winning. In one game against Yale University in the team's early days, an official unfairly called back a Carlisle **touchdown**. Despite protests by players and fans, the ruling stayed, and the Indians lost the game. The newspaper stories the next day all sided with Carlisle.

In addition to contending with unfair officials, Carlisle was outsized in most games. The heaviest Carlisle player was usually around 170 pounds, while most opponents had players that weighed more than 200 pounds. The Indians had to think of ways to win games other than with brute force—which was the method of the day. Carlisle learned to run legal, but trick, plays. "Nothing delighted [my players] more than to outsmart [their opponents]," Pop Warner said.

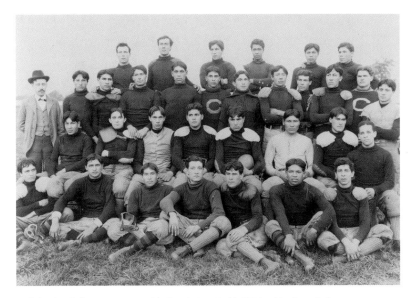

Carlisle's football program existed before Jim's arrival in 1904—this photo is from 1899—but he helped make the team one of the best in college football.

Jim's First Season

By the time Thorpe wanted to join the team in 1907, the Indians were at the top of their game. In the four previous seasons, Carlisle had a combined record of 39–11–1. The 1907 team was predicted to be its finest ever. Pop Warner, who had been away from Carlisle for the past three seasons, had returned as head coach in December 1906. "It was about as perfect a football machine as I've ever sent on the field," Warner said about the 1907 squad.

Once practice began in August, Thorpe begged Pop to let him try out for the team. "I want to play football," he insisted. Warner was reluctant to grant Jim's request. Although Thorpe had bulked up in the last couple years, Warner still thought he was too small for the rough game. Jim was also his track star, and Pop didn't want him to get injured. Thorpe, though, continued to beg the coach relentlessly.

"All right," Warner finally consented. "Go out there and give my varsity boys a little tackling practice. And believe me, that is all you'll be."

Pop tossed Thorpe the ball, and Jim took off. About thirty or so players tried to tackle him, but they all missed. Pop could not believe his eyes. He knew this boy could run on the track, but he thought the football field would be a different story. After all, Jim was taking on some of the best players in the nation.

Warner told Jim to try and run through his defense one more time. Once again, nobody came close to stopping him. Jim ran over to the sideline, tossed the ball to one of the assistant coaches, and stated confidently, "Nobody is going to tackle Jim!"

Warner had this to say: "Jim's performance at practice that afternoon was an exhibition of athletic talent that I had never before witnessed, nor was I ever to again see anything similar which might compare to it."

Pop could not believe his eyes. He knew this boy could run on the track, but he thought the football field would be a different story.

Thanks to this electrifying practice feat, Jim made the varsity squad right away. But Coach Warner thought his **rookie** still needed seasoning— time to learn the complexities of the game of football. Thus, Jim spent a lot of time on the bench in 1907. His role was to back up star **halfback** Albert Payne. Thorpe finally got onto the field in the seventh game of the year, against the University of Pennsylvania (Penn).

Pop Warner

When an NFL quarterback throws a brilliant 70-yard spiral, he should thank Pop Warner. Warner is one of the fathers of American football. He helped make the game what it is today. In addition to popularizing the spiral pass, he was famous for creating offensive schemes called the **single** and **double wing** attacks.

"I consider Warner to be the greatest creative genius in American football," said Andy Kerr, one of Pop's close friends and a fellow coach.

Born Glenn Scobey Warner in 1871, Pop loved sports from an early age. He attended Cornell University Law School in 1892, where he was introduced to football. He earned the nickname "Pop" at Cornell because he was older than most of the other guys on the team. After graduating in 1894, Pop practiced law briefly, but was soon bored. He wanted to try his hand at coaching football instead.

Warner made his way to Carlisle in 1899. "The Indian boys appealed to my football imagination," he said. Warner coached at Carlisle for thirteen seasons, 1899–1903 and 1907–1914. He went 113-42-8. In his forty-four-year overall stint as a head football coach, he won 318 games of 456.

The legendary Pop Warner coached college football for 44 years. This photo is from 1932, when he was the coach at Stanford University.

With all his football success, though, he was most famous for coaching the best athlete in the game. "When [Jim Thorpe] went all out," Pop once said, "it was humanly impossible for anyone to be better."

By this time in the season, the Indians were off to a 6–0 start. One of the biggest reasons they were undefeated was that they used the **passing game** as a strategy effectively. In 1906, the forward pass was made legal with the hope it would help cut back on injuries. Players wore little or no padding, and the game was very violent. In the 1905 season alone, there were eighteen deaths reported among college football players. The thinking was that the passing game would open up the field and keep players from crashing into one another as often.

Most teams, though, still did not use the forward pass much or at all. The Indians were an exception. Warner had even taught his quarterback to "scramble." After receiving the ball from the center, he ran a few yards to his left or right to avoid would-be tacklers. This also gave his receivers time to get downfield to receive a pass. All quarterbacks today use this type of movement, but back in 1906 it was a new concept. Carlisle was now a triple threat: the team could run, pass, or kick out of its initial formation. This meant they could surprise the opposing team, who would not know how to defend against them.

Carlisle was now a triple threat: the team could run, pass, or kick out of its initial formation. This meant they could surprise their opposing team, who would not know how to defend against them.

Against Pennsylvania in front of 22,000 fans, the Indians looked unstoppable. Thorpe got his chance to play when Payne injured his knee. On Thorpe's first run, he ran the exact opposite way of his blockers and was buried by tacklers. The next time he touched the ball, though, he sprinted 75 yards and scored a touchdown.

Above is a photograph of Jim in his Carlisle football uniform. Although Carlisle won 10 of 11 games in 1907, Jim was not a big star—yet.

Carlisle went on to win the game easily, 26–6, and finished the season at 10–1. The team's only loss of the season came against Princeton University, when the rainy weather made the ball slick and difficult to pass. Although Jim played in the remainder of the games and played well, he was not yet the big star he would become. Captain Albert Exendine was named second-team All-America, but Thorpe received no national honors. When asked later in his life about the 1907 season, Thorpe had only this to say: "I didn't like it much on the bench."

It wouldn't much matter. Jim Thorpe would not sit there for any stretch of time again—especially if the fans had anything to do with it.

CHAPTER 4

Becoming a Star

There seemed nothing he could not do.

—Pop Warner

The chant could be heard across Indian Field, home of Carlisle's football team. "We want Jim! We want Jim!" the crowd roared over and over again. It was the third game of the Indians' 1908 football season. The game was scoreless in the second half in a matchup against Villanova University. Over the course of one summer, Jim Thorpe had blossomed into the team's star halfback. Now he was sitting on the bench. Head coach Pop Warner had not put his star in the game for fear he would be injured and not be able to play against tougher teams later in the season. Carlisle had easily won its first two games—53–0 over a **prep school** for Dickinson College and 35–0 over Lebanon Valley College. Villanova was Carlisle's last "easy" opponent before it hit the road to face the traditional football powers such as Yale and Harvard Universities.

Warner finally relented to the crowd's pleas and sent Jim onto the field. Thorpe took the first handoff and blasted through Villanova's defensive line with the ball. He blew through their **backfield** without a single block and ran into the **end zone** for a 70-yard touchdown. Villanova's spirit was officially broken. Coach Warner quickly took Jim out of the game again so as not to risk injury. The Indians went on to win 10–0.

Harvard and Yale usually ranked among the best college football teams of the early 1900s. This photograph is from when they played each other in 1908. To this day, the annual Harvard-Yale game is one of football's biggest rivalry events.

Jim, age twenty-one, no longer belonged on the bench—in fact, he was star of the show now, and not just on the football field. The previous spring, Jim had again been the standout on the school's track team. Coach Warner asked Jim to perform in many different events—wherever they needed to pick up points—and Jim almost always won. At the Middle Atlantic Association Meet in Philadelphia, where all the top college athletes were competing, Jim won the hammer throw, the high and low hurdles, and the high and long jumps. "There seemed nothing he could not do," Coach Warner said about Jim's performances.

Jim was no longer a boy but a man with a strong personality. He had inherited his father's temper, which sometimes flared up if Pop Warner pushed him too hard. Although Jim excelled in competition, he wasn't especially motivated to do his best all the time. He performed overconfidently at times, which frustrated his coaches and teammates. "He wanted to win, but that was enough," said teammate Albert Exendine. "In races, he sometimes took the last hurdle far in front and then just strolled across the finish line."

After the track-and-field season ended, Jim's natural athletic ability allowed him to walk onto Carlisle's baseball team. He pitched a couple of games at the end of the Indians' 27-game season, including a 1–0 **shutout** over Albright College.

Jim went home for summer vacation after baseball ended. He visited with siblings, and then returned to Carlisle early. Football season and the new school year were still a month away. Jim used the month to train for football. When the season arrived, he was a well-oiled machine.

"There seemed nothing he could not do," Coach Warner said about Jim's performances.

On the Road

From the first kickoff, Jim was clearly the star of Carlisle's 1908 team. In addition to playing halfback, he was a standout **placekicker** and **punter**. The most memorable game of the season came against the University of Pennsylvania Quakers on October 24. Some 26,000 fans in Philadelphia witnessed one of the fiercest defensive battles played. Penn had two All-Americas on its team who were the toughest tacklers in the game. Thorpe described being leveled by one of them as feeling like he'd been hit by a "battering ram."

Penn scored the first touchdown of the game, but in the second half, Thorpe figured out a way to show off his skills. On a run from the Quakers' 40-yard line, he exploded through an opening between defenders. Then, when he was just about

Jim could do it all on a football field, including kick. In this photo, he showcases his drop-kicking skill. (The ball hits the ground an instant before it is kicked.)

to be tackled, he hurled himself across the goal line for the touchdown. The game ended in a tie, 6–6. Carlisle was the only team to tie the undefeated Quakers the entire season. Jim later called this matchup "the toughest game in my twenty-two years of college and professional football."

Carlisle finished the season with a 10–2–1 record. Its two losses came against Harvard (17–0) and the University of Minnesota (11–6). Despite its shutout win over Carlisle, Harvard fans and players were still wowed by Thorpe's athletic prowess. On one play, Jim sliced and diced through the defensive line, cut to the outside, and sprinted up the sideline for 65 yards, where he was caught at the 8-yard line, just outside the end zone. At the time, the young Indian was playing on a sprained ankle.

The game ended in a tie, 6–6. Carlisle was the only team to tie the undefeated Quakers the entire season.

"When you're talking about Big Jim's football ability," Vic Choctaw Kelley, one of Jim's 1908 teammates, exclaimed, "you can't exaggerate. He was the greatest, that's all."

When the season ended, Jim had been named to the third-highest All-America team of national college all-stars. But he and his teammates were exhausted. They were tired not only from the physical play, but the travel as well. Most colleges, due to racist motives, refused to play "the Indian school" anywhere but on their home turf. Thus, Pop Warner's bunch had played ten of its thirteen games on the road. In the last five games of the season, the team traveled 5,000 miles by train over twenty-two straight days. All this travel exhausted the players. Not even professional baseball players, the only pro team players at the time, traveled as much in such a short span.

Jim rested up over the Christmas break, then came back ready to excel on the track team. His greatest performance of the season came against Lafayette College, a meet in which he won six events—the 120-yard hurdles, 220-yard low hurdles, long jump, high jump, shot put, and discus—and finished third in another—the 100 meters. Lafayette's track coach at the time, Harold Anson Bruce, had this to say: "Jim just picked up things and did it. Everything came natural."

"The Natural" ended his 1909 track season almost routinely—he won five more events in a meet against Syracuse University.

Summer Baseball

Despite his success on the track, Jim loved to play baseball far more than he loved running. One reason was that he dreamed of getting paid to play one day. At the time, baseball was the only major professional sport in the United States. Warner, though, tried to discourage Jim's dream of playing professional baseball. Selfishly, he loved having Thorpe as his track star. Jim complained: "What's the use of bothering with all this [track] stuff? There is [no money] in it."

When the 1908–1909 school year ended, Jim seized an opportunity to play baseball for pay. A couple of schoolmates of his were heading down to North Carolina to play in a semiprofessional minor league, and Jim decided to tag along. The three Carlisle boys joined the Rocky Mount Railroaders. There were thirty-five minor leagues to choose from in 1909. The Railroaders, in the Eastern Carolina League, were the worst team in their league. Thorpe was offered fifteen to twenty-five dollars a week to play—not a lot, even then. Jim was still excited to make money doing something he loved, and he accepted it eagerly.

Jim was far from being the star of the dismal Railroaders. In 44 games for Rocky Mount, his **batting average** was .253. Anything above .300 is considered good. He also had a losing record as a pitcher, winning 9 games and losing 10. He did shine

Amateur Versus Professional

An amateur athlete is one that plays for free, or does not accept payment for his or her performances. A professional player gets paid to play. A semipro player gets paid to play on a part-time basis. In 1909, just as today, college athletes were considered amateurs, and were not allowed to accept payments. Olympic athletes at that time were also considered amateurs.

When Jim Thorpe and his teammates accepted money to play for the Rocky Mount Railroaders, a minor-league team, technically they gave up their right to play as amateurs again. Thorpe was not even aware of this rule at the time.

as a base runner, though. Opponents reported that Jim was so fast, he was already standing on first base before they even picked up his hard-hit ground ball.

No matter how he played, Jim enjoyed his newfound freedom. He had lived in and out of boarding schools for the past seventeen years. Now, he could eat, sleep, and go out whenever he wanted—all he had to do was show up for games. At times, this led to some trouble for "Big Jim." He sometimes drank too much and got into fights at the local bar.

. . . Jim enjoyed his newfound freedom. . . . he could eat, sleep, and go out whenever he wanted—all he had to do was show up for games.

When the season ended, Jim couldn't bear the thought of returning to the disciplined life that Carlisle required. Instead, he decided to head back to Oklahoma once again. His sister

This picture is of a typical semipro baseball team, like the one on which Jim played in North Carolina. (The player standing at the far right, A. B. "Happy" Chandler, eventually became a United States senator and was the Commissioner of Baseball from 1945 to 1951.)

Mary had a farm, and in exchange for some farmwork, she offered him room and board.

Back on the Farm

Jim spent the fall of 1909 in Oklahoma. He felt like he was on vacation again—living without the school structure he had grown to resent.

Pop Warner felt like his star player had abandoned him. The coach was worried enough about the future of his team to try to get him back. In the two seasons Jim was away from Carlisle, the football team was noticeably weaker. In 1909, they lost to

Pop Warner (standing, far right) watches his Carlisle team practice. Warner was a great coach, but his teams were noticeably weaker without Jim Thorpe in 1909 and 1910.

Penn for the first time in four years and fell to the University of Pittsburgh (Pitt) for the first time ever. In 1910, they finished with a record of 8–6. It was Pop Warner's worst record as a head coach since 1901.

Pop invited Jim to come see Carlisle take on St. Louis University in the final game of the football season. Inspired by Thorpe's presence in the stands, the Indians won 32–0. After the game, Warner invited Thorpe to go hunting with him for a couple days. While on the trip, the coach hoped he could convince Thorpe to come back to school. Although Thorpe did come back to Carlisle—to visit around Christmastime—that was all.

When springtime rolled around, Jim once again returned to the East Carolina League—he played half the season for the Railroaders and the other half for the Fayetteville Highlanders.

His hitting was unremarkable: he batted .242 in a combined average for both teams. (He did forge a combined 10–10 record as a pitcher, though.) The most memorable moment of the season came when Jim was hit in the head by a thrown ball while trying to steal a base. Blood poured from his head. The crowd let out a collective gasp, but according to newspaper reports of the day, "The Big Indian sat down and laughed."

The season ended with Jim recovering in the hospital and with the news that the league was shutting down. It had run out of money.

Jim returned home once again to his sister Mary's farm. He stayed for more than a year, but eventually he began to feel restless and unfocused.

Thorpe's luck, though, was about to change for the better. In the summer of 1911, on the street in Anadarko, a village about fifty miles southwest of Oklahoma City, Jim bumped into one of his old pals and schoolmates, Albert Exendine. "Ex" was about to change Thorpe's life for the better.

> *Jim returned home once again to his sister Mary's farm. He stayed for more than a year, but eventually he began to feel restless and unfocused.*

CHAPTER 5

All-America

*I played for fun. I always have, ever since I was
a kid.*

Albert Exendine, having graduated from Carlisle and
Dickinson Law School, was the head football coach
at Otterbein College in Ohio. He was back in Oklahoma
visiting with relatives and checking on family property. On
the day Ex ran into his old teammate, Thorpe was feeling
lost and directionless. His semipro baseball days were
behind him, and he didn't know what he wanted to do
next with his life.

Despite these frustrations, Jim was still glad to see his
old pal. He charged over to shake Albert's hand. When Ex
spotted his old buddy coming toward him, he couldn't
believe how thick Jim had become. Standing 5 feet
11 inches and weighing 185 pounds, Thorpe was about
25 pounds heavier than he'd been as a student at Carlisle.

Talking under the afternoon sun, Ex and Jim chatted
about all the fun they had had at Carlisle together. Ex
suggested to Jim that he return to school in the fall and
play football again. "They wouldn't want me there now,"
Jim replied.

"You bet they would," Albert responded.

Both young men were actually right. On the one
side, head football coach Pop Warner desperately
wanted Jim back. His teams were just mediocre without
Thorpe, and he wanted Carlisle to be great again. But

The Carlisle team plays Georgetown University during Jim Thorpe's time. At Albert Exendine's urging, Jim returned to the team in 1911 after missing the previous two seasons.

the superintendent of the school, Moses Friedman, had grown frustrated with Jim's behavior. Jim was a weak student and had earned a reputation for drinking too much alcohol. Plus, Thorpe had already run away from Carlisle one too many times. Friedman was simply tired of the young man's attitude.

In the end, though, money talked. Friedman realized if Thorpe could make the football team good again, it would help bring in a lot of cash from ticket sales. The school always needed money just to stay afloat.

Soon after Jim ran into Ex, he received a letter from Warner. In the letter, Pop invited Jim back to Carlisle in time to play for the 1911 squad. Pop also tried to entice Jim back to school with another promise. He told his star athlete that he would help him train to make the 1912 U.S. Olympic Team. Jim couldn't resist such an offer to compete against the world's best. He arrived back on campus in September 1911.

Tour de Thorpe

When Thorpe returned to Carlisle, it was like he'd never left. If anything, his football skills seemed to have improved with the time off, not diminished. He was faster, stronger, and more skilled than anybody else on the field. At age twenty-four, Jim found that the game came more naturally to him than ever. "He was born a football player," Warner said about Thorpe.

He was faster, stronger, and more skilled than anybody else on the field.

Warner treated Jim differently than he had before as well. Pop had a temper, and he spent a lot of practice yelling at his players. In fact, he got so mad one time that he punched one of his athletes. This time around, though, he rarely yelled at Jim. He learned from seasons past that Jim did not respond to verbal threats. In fact, they made him play worse, not better. When Jim loafed through practice drills, Warner would not say a word. Instead, he counted on Jim to step up his play when game time arrived. The strategy proved to be effective.

Jim helped Carlisle win in the first game of the season, a 53–0 blowout over Lebanon Valley. He also played in the following game against Muhlenberg College. Thorpe punished the Muhlenberg defense, carrying the ball on almost every play. Sometimes he ran around the defense, but many times he just mowed a player down. On one of his runs, he plowed into a player so hard that he broke the defender's collarbone.

"It was the first time I was glad to be taken out of a game," the Muhlenberg player recalled.

Carlisle won that game 32–0 and beat Dickinson 17–0 the following week. The highlight of the Dickinson game came when Thorpe ran 85 yards for a touchdown. An article in the *New York Times* called the run the "feature of the contest."

One of the techniques Thorpe used to avoid getting tackled was called the "stiff-arm." As Thorpe ran, he held the football under one arm. Then, when a defender came near him, he would swing his free arm down as hard as he could and nail the defender in the forehead before the player could even get his hands on Jim. (The game was rougher back then compared to today's standards.)

This photograph shows an example of a stiff-arm, a tactic that Jim used to his advantage during his football career. The Tampa Bay ball carrier, Carnell Williams, fends off the Carolina Panthers player who is trying to tackle him in this NFL game in 2005.

The Indians won their fourth game over Mount St. Mary's University 46–5, and trounced Georgetown University 28–5. Next up was Pittsburgh, where twelve thousand fans filled Pitt's stadium to watch the Indians play. According to reports of the day, Thorpe ran a play against Pitt that left fans stunned. In the second quarter, Carlisle faced a fourth down deep in its own territory. This meant they had only one play left to get the ball farther down the field, or Pittsburgh would get the ball dangerously close to the Indians' end zone. Thorpe lined up to punt (he was also the team's best kicker). He punted the ball high into the air. When no Pittsburgh player blocked him, Thorpe chased the punt. (The rules of the game at the time stated that either team could catch a punt and try to advance it for their team.) Thorpe blasted up the field and made it before the ball landed. Three Pitt players and Thorpe leaped into the air at the same time to try to catch the ball, but Thorpe leaped the highest. He snagged the ball, then ran over 20 more yards for the touchdown. Carlisle went on to win the game that day, 17–0. Newspaper reports called Thorpe the greatest athlete ever and stated that he seemed to possess "superhuman speed."

Three Pitt players and Thorpe leaped into the air at the same time to try to catch the ball, but Thorpe leaped the highest. He snagged the ball, then ran over 20 more yards for the touchdown.

The heroics of Jim Thorpe were becoming more and more legendary with every single game. With that, the pressure for him to perform became greater as well. Jim, though, did not get caught up in his hype. He just went out and played. "I played for fun," Thorpe said about that season. "I always have, ever since I was a kid."

Playing through Pain

After Carlisle beat Pitt, its record for the 1911 football season stood a perfect 5–0. The next week, the Indians easily beat Lafayette 19–0, but they also suffered a serious setback. Thorpe severely twisted his ankle during the game and had to sit out the next week's match versus the University of Pennsylvania. (Carlisle still won 16–0.) The week after the Penn game, Carlisle faced its toughest rival, Harvard. Harvard was a football powerhouse back then. The Indians had beaten Harvard just once in twelve tries since 1896. If they were to stand a chance this season, Coach Warner knew Thorpe had to play.

The week leading up to the big game, Coach Warner spent hours massaging and tending to Thorpe's ankle with ointments and vibrating machines. But when game time arrived, Thorpe's ankle was still in bad shape. Thorpe hated to miss any games and desperately wanted to play. So, Warner wrapped it the best he could in adhesive plaster, and sent him out to the field to start at halfback. Thorpe wanted to play through the pain.

But when game time arrived, Thorpe's ankle was still in bad shape.

With Thorpe limping and Carlisle seriously outnumbered (Harvard had 50 men on its sidelines, the Indians had just 16), it looked as if Carlisle's perfect season would soon end. In fact, Harvard's head coach wasn't even taking his opponent seriously and wasn't at the game. He had gone to Yale for the afternoon to scout their team. (Harvard was scheduled to face Yale the following week.)

The Carlisle team members were insulted that they were taken so lightly. Injury or no injury, Thorpe and the Indians were now motivated to show the crowd just how good they were.

This photograph shows one of Carlisle's great teams from Jim's era. He's standing in the middle of the top row.

In the first half, Thorpe kicked two successful **field goals** with his injured foot, but Harvard still led 9–6. In the second half, Carlisle scored a touchdown, and Thorpe booted another successful field goal to help Carlisle take a 15–9 lead. Pop Warner could not have felt more proud of his star's performance: "Although every movement must have been agony," Warner said, "not once did he take a time-out."

Bandaged ankle and all, Thorpe ran for 173 yards in the second half, but never once into the end zone for a touchdown. He kicked another field goal though, and the game ended in Carlisle's favor, 18–15. As the clock ran out, Thorpe was carried off the field by teammates. The Harvard fans cheered for him in amazement. The *Boston American*, a newspaper, printed this about Thorpe's performance: "He has placed his name in the Hall of Fame, not only of Carlisle, but also of the entire football world."

After such an emotional victory, Carlisle had trouble gearing up for the following week's game versus Syracuse. Playing in the wind and the rain, the Indians played poorly and suffered their first and only loss of the season, 12–11. Jim was still in pain from his ankle injury and also never played well in bad weather. He had one of his worst games of the year, missing an extra point that could have tied the game.

The Indians recovered and won their last two games of the season to finish at 11–1. Thorpe was named a first-team All-America halfback, earning one of college sports' highest honors.

Despite being beat up and tired by the season's end, Thorpe enjoyed the winter at Carlisle. He competed in track, breaking the school's high-jump record with a leap of 6 feet 1 inch. Thorpe also enjoyed a busy social life. He loved going to school dances and was quite a graceful dancer. One of his dance partners at the time was fellow student Iva Miller, who would eventually become his first wife. At the time, Iva was known as the prettiest girl at Carlisle.

Iva Miller

Iva Margaret Miller, nicknamed Ivy, was Jim's first wife. They were married on October 14, 1913. Ivy, who was six years younger than Jim, was also born in Indian Territory in Oklahoma. But unlike other students at Carlisle, Ivy was barely Indian. Her father, Finas Miller, was white, and her mother, Mattie Denton, was mostly white, with just a tiny bit of Cherokee blood. Like Thorpe's parents at the time he met her, Ivy's parents had died—hers when she was five. Despite Ivy's lack of Indian heritage, her aunt, Grace Miller, who was a teacher at Carlisle and Ivy's guardian, managed to get her into Carlisle because she was such a stellar student. (Under Carlisle rules, students were supposed to be at least one-quarter Indian.) In 1912, Ivy graduated from Carlisle with a degree in sewing.

In the spring of 1912, Jim began training exclusively for that summer's Olympic Games in Stockholm, Sweden. This photo was taken just a few weeks before the Games began.

That spring, Thorpe once again dominated the outdoor track season. But he had his eyes set upon bigger goals than just winning for Carlisle. He was getting ready for the 1912 Summer Olympics.

In late April, Coach Warner took Thorpe, and his track team pal Louis Tewanima, away from Carlisle and back to his home in Springville, New York. Although competing at school helped them prepare, Warner wanted to help "his boys" get ready for the Games without any distractions. According to Warner, both men were such standouts at Carlisle, they were named to the U.S. team without having to try out.

CHAPTER 6

Olympic Glory

I had trained well and hard and had confidence in my ability. I felt that I would win.

Jim Thorpe could not believe his eyes. It was a warm Friday morning on June 14, 1912. He had finished training for the Olympics the previous spring. Now, he was about to board the SS *Finland*—a ship that would carry the U.S. Olympic Team to the Games in Stockholm, Sweden. The ship was massive—560 feet long—and Thorpe was astounded something that size could float. "I'd never seen a boat as big as that before," he said. "Nothing was like it—walking on the boat, and all those cabins and decks and eating and sleeping on it!"

Thorpe and Tewanima, along with their coach, Pop Warner, were traveling with 177 U.S. athletes to compete in the sixth Summer Olympic Games. Jim would compete in the decathlon and pentathlon while Lewis would run the 10,000 meters (6.2 miles) and the marathon (26.2 miles). In many ways,

This is an official poster from the 1912 Olympic Games in Stockholm. It is on display at the Olympic Museum in Lausanne, Switzerland.

History of the Modern Olympics

The ancient Olympics began in 776 B.C. in Greece, but were banned by a Roman emperor in 393 A.D. The modern Olympic Games were the brainchild of a Frenchman named Baron Pierre de Coubertin, who believed in the goodness of sports. The first modern Olympics were held in Athens, Greece, in 1896. Seventy-four athletes from eleven countries joined 102 competitors from Greece in mid-April. The athletes competed as individuals, not as representatives of their country. The United States dominated the track-and-field events—winning nine of the twelve. The winners were awarded silver medals, not gold ones. Second-place finishers were awarded bronze medals, and third-place finishers were not awarded anything. Athletes were first awarded gold, silver, and bronze medals at the 1904 Games in St. Louis, Missouri.

Since 1896, summer competition has been held every four years, with the exception of skipping 1916 for World War I, and 1940 and 1944 for World War II. The Winter Games began in 1924 and have been held every four years with the exception of 1940 and 1944 as well. In 1992 and 1994, the Winter Olympics were held two years apart so that the Summer and Winter Games would run in different years.

Baron Pierre de Coubertin was the visionary behind the modern Olympic Games. He revived the ancient tradition in Athens, Greece, in 1896.

The Olympics today are bigger than ever. At the 2008 Summer Games in Beijing, more than 10,000 athletes from 205 countries competed.

Jim had been training for such a competition his whole life. As a boy in Oklahoma, he'd spent his days running, jumping, and throwing—which is exactly what he'd be doing at the Olympics.

Although Tewanima didn't have to try out at all for the Olympic team, and Thorpe didn't for the decathlon, Jim did have to show off his athletic skills in the pentathlon. The event was being contested for the first time. The tryouts were held on May 18, 1912, in New York City. According to the *New York Times*, Thorpe proved to be "in a class by himself," winning the 200-meter sprint, the running long jump, and the discus, while placing second in the javelin and the 1,500-meter run. He was clearly the best in the United States.

Once the Carlisle students and the other athletes were on the boat to the Olympic Games, they were permitted the day to unpack and get settled. As the ship pulled out of port, 5,000 supporters waved American flags and shouted their good wishes from the shore. All the athletes, including Thorpe, waved back enthusiastically, enjoying the big send-off. Soon after the vessel was at sea, though, life turned to all business. The athletes had a full schedule of training to follow on their ten-day voyage across the Atlantic Ocean. Beginning at 10:30 a.m. every day, each athlete worked on his sport: runners such as Tewanima circled the ship on

The athletes had a full schedule of training to follow on their ten-day voyage across the Atlantic Ocean.

an eighth-of-a-mile cork track, swimmers swam in canvas tanks, and tennis players swatted the ball against the wall for hours on end. Although Thorpe did train along with the other athletes, he also spent quite a bit of time sitting alone on the deck and visualizing. One day, a reporter from New York's *Evening Mail* spotted Jim sitting this way. "What are you doing, Jim?" the reporter asked as Thorpe sat in a deck chair.

"I'm practicing the long jump," Jim responded. "I've just jumped twenty-three feet, eight inches. I think that I can win it."

Let the Games Begin

The SS *Finland* arrived first in Antwerp, Belgium. The U.S. athletes trained there for three more days, then re-boarded the ship for a four-day passage to Stockholm. According to reports, Jim was quiet for most of the ride—he sat staring out the window, perhaps imagining what he planned to do in competition.

Once in Stockholm, most of the other athletes got back on board the *Finland* to live there during the Games. Pop Warner took Thorpe and Tewanima to a private residence in Stocksund,

This photograph is from the Opening Ceremonies of the 1912 Olympics. The Swedish National Team marches into Stockholm Stadium.

about twenty-five miles outside Stockholm. He wanted his boys to focus on training, just as he did before the Games, without outside distractions from other athletes.

The Opening Ceremonies were held on July 6. More than 30,000 fans were on hand to watch the 2,405 athletes from twenty-eight countries march onto the field in the center of the new Stockholm Olympic Stadium. For the first time, athletes were competing for their country, not just as individuals. The temperature soared to well above ninety degrees that day. Thorpe knew the hot weather was in his favor—after all, unlike athletes from other parts of the world, he'd grown up running all day long under the hot sun on the Oklahoma plains.

The pentathlon began on the second day of competition. The first event was the long jump. Jim's winning jump measured 23 feet $2^{7}/_{10}$ inches—close to the distance he pictured while relaxing on the ship. Next up was the javelin throw, where Jim's form was raw at best. He had had little training and had only been throwing the spear for a couple of weeks. He still managed to finish third—thanks to his brute strength. The third event of the day was the 200-meter race. Thorpe won in a nail-biter, pulling ahead of the other six pentathletes with barely ten

Jim throws the discus during competition at the 1912 Olympics. He won gold medals in both the decathlon and the pentathlon.

Jim crosses the finish line ahead of the pack in the 1,500-meter run during the pentathlon at the Olympic Games. He went on to finish first overall in the five-event competition, too.

meters to go. When the competition ended for the day, Thorpe was in first place overall. The next day, the final two events, the discus and the 1,500 meters, were contested. Jim won the discus—his throw was three feet farther than that of the second-place finisher, Avery Brundage. Thorpe made his move in the 1,500-meter race in the second lap, when he passed Brundage and a competitor from Norway, Ferdinand Bie. The two never caught him, and Jim finished in a time of 4 minutes 44.8 seconds. Thorpe's dominance in the pentathlon had been spectacular. For each event, athletes were awarded 1 point for first place, 2 points for second, and so on, so Thorpe's score of 7 points beat Bie's 21. Now an Olympic champion, Thorpe had six days to rest up for the ten-event decathlon.

Dominating in Decathlon

On Saturday, July 13, 1912, the decathlon competition got under way. Jim had spent the previous week training a little and lying in a hammock, but also entering some individual track events. Although he had not done particularly well—he finished fourth in the open division of high jump and seventh in the long jump—he just loved being part of the action. "What's the fun of watching someone else?" Thorpe asked one of the Olympic coaches. He did, however, enjoy watching his friend Lewis Tewanima win a silver medal in the 10,000 meters. (Lewis finished sixteenth in the marathon.)

Despite Jim's dominating performance in the pentathlon, sportswriters expected a Swedish athlete named Hugo Wieslander to win the decathlon. This was the first time the

decathlon competition was being held in the Olympics. Wieslander had competed in three decathlons, thus giving him the most experience, and what people thought was the edge to win.

The first day of competition was wet and rainy, which did not bode well for Thorpe: he loved sunny weather and competed at his worst in wet conditions. (In the few rainy-day football games Thorpe had experienced at Carlisle, he'd played poorly.) After finishing second in the 100 meters, Jim stepped over the takeoff board on his first

With gold medals in two premier events, Jim was the star of the 1912 Olympics.

Decathlon Today

The decathlon events of today have not changed since Jim Thorpe competed. There are still ten events held over a two-day period (at the 1912 Games, the competition was held over three days because of the large number of participants). On the first day, the athletes compete in the 100-meter dash, long jump, shot put, high jump, and 400-meter run. These events focus on speed, power, and jumping ability. The next day the athletes compete in the 110-meter hurdles, discus throw, pole vault, javelin throw, and 1,500-meter run. These events emphasize technical skill and endurance.

Jim Thorpe was the first of a long line of Americans to win the competition that identifies the "World's Greatest Athlete." In fact, an American has won twelve of the twenty-three Olympic decathlon gold medals to date. Most recently, Bryan Clay, an athlete who grew up in Hawaii, won at the 2008 Games in Beijing, China. Like Thorpe, Clay was dominant. His point total was 8,791—240 points better than silver medalist Andrei Krauchanka of Belarus. It was the largest winning margin since 1972.

The winner of the Olympic decathlon is called the "World's Greatest Athlete." American Bryan Clay (pictured) earned that title at the 2008 Games in Beijing.

The judges eyed Jim as he pursued a gold medal in the decathlon several days after winning the title in the pentathlon.

two jumps of the long jump. If he did it again, it would mean no score, and most likely no chance of winning the decathlon. As Thorpe stood at the end of the runway, he looked perfectly calm. He took off and made a clean jump, landing at a distance of 22 feet 2³/₁₀ inches. The jump was good for second place and enough to keep Jim vying for the gold. In the last event of the day, the shot put, Jim finished second as well. Although he had not won an event that day, his point total was enough to give him a bit of a lead over his competitors.

On the second day of the three-day event, the weather was bright and sunny—and Jim finished first in the high jump and the 110-meter hurdles, and second in the 400-meter run and the discus. The third day, another clear one with no rain, Jim finished third in the pole vault, fourth in the javelin, and ended the competition with a win in the 1,500 meters—close to five seconds faster than his time in the pentathlon.

The grueling event was over . . . and Jim Thorpe had won, far ahead of the expected winner, Wieslander. Perhaps at times Thorpe looked as if he could be defeated, but he never felt this way. "I had trained well and hard and had confidence in my ability," he said. "I felt that I would win."

> *The grueling event was over . . . and Jim Thorpe had won, . . .*

Thorpe's decathlon victory set a world record that would stand for sixteen years. He also became the only athlete in Olympic history to win both the decathlon and the pentathlon (the pentathlon, different from the modern pentathlon, which includes horseback riding, shooting, and fencing, was dropped after the 1924 Games).

The decathlon was the last event of the Games. On the day it concluded, the final awards ceremony was also held. Sweden's King Gustav V awarded Jim two gold medals, as well as a laurel wreath to put atop his head. The king shook Thorpe's hand and said the line that would become linked to Jim's name for the rest of his life: "Sir, you are the greatest athlete in the world."

Gustav V was the king of Sweden from 1907 until his death in 1950. He congratulated Thorpe after his historic performance at the Olympics.

CHAPTER 7

A Hero's Welcome

You have covered yourself with glory.
    —*Moses Friedman*

Once again, Jim Thorpe could not believe his eyes. It was August 16, 1912, and the Olympic hero was back in the United States. He had just arrived at the train station in Carlisle, Pennsylvania, where banners hung from the walls, all in praise of Thorpe, Coach Pop Warner, and Louis Tewanima. They said things such as HAIL TO CHIEF THORPE and, for Pop Warner THE GREATEST COACH IN THE WORLD.

After winning his two gold medals, Thorpe had spent a month in Europe with other members of the American team. They competed in a series of post-Olympic meets in Paris and Reims, France, where Thorpe beat Olympic gold medalist Fred Kelly in the 110-meter high hurdles. Most of the other athletes were worn out and performed poorly— not Jim. His performance was

After the Olympic Games, members of the American track team competed in Europe. Jim is pictured in Reims, France, in this photo.

After the Olympics, Jim was as famous as the president of the United States, William Howard Taft, who is pictured here.

top rate, despite his having to endure the most attention and pressure from the crowds. He was the fan favorite of all the athletes. "Thorpe held up the best," Abel Kivet, a U.S. runner who won silver in the 1,500 meters, said. "And he was under the most strain," Kivet added, referring to the pressure of meeting everyone's high expectations.

As soon as Jim arrived back in the United States after the post-Olympic meets, he took the train back to school. Jim was now a national hero. Newspapers included as many stories about him as they did about the president of the United States, William Howard Taft. Little boys and girls all wanted Jim's autograph.

Upon arriving in Carlisle, Jim, Coach Warner, and Lewis Tewanima headed to Biddle Field at Dickinson College for a Welcome Home rally. A band played, fire engines blared their sirens, speeches were made, and more than 5,000 fans cheered for the Olympians. The superintendent of the Carlisle School, Moses Friedman, was the first to shower Jim with praise. "We welcome you, James Thorpe, to this town and back to your school," Friedman said. "You have covered yourself with glory." These congratulations meant a lot to Jim coming from a man who once thought he had a poor attitude.

A couple of days after the celebration in Carlisle, the trio traveled to New York City for the biggest parade Jim had ever seen. The U.S. Olympians traveled down Fifth Avenue in open-air cars, while more than a million people waved from

Back at Carlisle, Jim got a warm welcome. In this photo, he's shaking hands with Moses Friedman, the superintendent of the school.

the sidewalks. "I never knew one person could have so many friends," Thorpe said with awe.

Thorpe wasn't used to all this attention—witnesses said he seemed uncomfortable that day. He pulled his white-brimmed hat down over his eyes many times during the parade—perhaps in shyness. This was the same man, after all, who was born to humble means in a one-room cabin.

A couple of days after the New York parade, Jim and the other athletes appeared center stage at a rally for Olympians in Philadelphia. After the rally, Jim returned to the Carlisle School. He was a big-time star, but he still had to figure out what he wanted to do with his life. He was just twenty-five years old, and his choices seemed limitless.

Back to Carlisle

Once the Olympic celebration settled down around him, Jim received offers from practically everywhere. Professional baseball teams tried to sign Jim by tempting him with huge contracts. A boxing promoter tried to get him to step into the ring. A horse-racing promoter wanted Jim to race a horse. Several track coaches even tried to get Jim to compete in meets across the country. Jim was overwhelmed by all his choices. He turned for advice to the one person he trusted the most: Pop Warner.

Although Pop Warner did want the best for Jim, he also wanted what was best for himself, and this meant Jim coming back to Carlisle. Pop was convinced that if Jim came and played one more season, the Indians would win the national title. He also told Jim if he did help lead Carlisle to

Although Pop Warner did want the best for Jim, he also wanted what was best for himself, and this meant Jim coming back to Carlisle.

Jim was back on the football field for Carlisle not long after his amazing Olympic performance. In this photo, he's warming up before a game in 1912.

the title, he'd have even more opportunities to make money after the football season ended.

Convinced Pop had his best interests at heart, Jim decided to return. But this decision meant it would be a struggle again to live by all the school's rules—especially after becoming an Olympic hero. "I have the chance to make a bunch of dough after leaving this school," Jim wrote in a letter to his half-brother, Frank. "It's hard to go back again, but it is for my good, so I will make the best of things."

With Jim back on the squad, Carlisle crushed the first four "warm-up" teams on its 1912 schedule—Albright College (50–7), Lebanon Valley (45–0), Dickinson (34–0), and Villanova (65–0). In the Villanova game, Thorpe scored three touchdowns in less than 30 minutes of action. The Indians were averaging close to 50 points a game and seemed unstoppable. That is, until they met Washington and Jefferson College in Washington, Pennsylvania.

A Sign of Trouble

In this game, Thorpe had four **interceptions**, but he never scored a touchdown. He also missed four field goals. Until now, he had rarely missed even one. The game, played in front of 10,000 fans, ended in a 0–0 tie.

Thorpe and his teammates were visibly upset after the game. Jim and one of his pals on the team snuck off to a bar to drown their sorrows in beer. When Coach Warner found out, he was furious. He went to the bar and tried to force Jim to leave, but Thorpe refused. Pop recruited some of his other players, and they forcibly put Jim on the train to go home.

The next day, Warner yelled at his star player. He told him his behavior was not suitable for an Olympic champion or, for that matter, a Carlisle football player. This incident, though, wasn't just a mistake by Thorpe. It also revealed a much more complicated side of the young man.

Although Jim was a great athlete, he had conflicting feelings about being in the spotlight and all the pressure to succeed that fell on his shoulders. At times, the pressure became too much to handle. Although it wasn't a healthy or smart choice, Jim found that drinking helped him deal with that pressure. In the end, Jim apologized to his coach and his teammates and even promised not to drink again (although he would not keep that promise). Pop and Jim simply tried to put the embarrassing incident behind them.

Syracuse was next up on the schedule. The Orangemen had been the only team to defeat the Indians the previous season, but Carlisle easily won 33–0 this time around, then went on to beat Pittsburgh 45–8 and Georgetown 34–20. After beating Georgetown, the Indians traveled to Toronto, Canada, to face off against some of Canada's top rugby players. The first half was played by U.S. football rules, the second half was played by Canadian rugby rules. Carlisle won this international matchup 49–1.

Next up was Lehigh University, whom Carlisle beat 34–14. Victories were coming so easily to Carlisle that its players felt confident enough to joke around on the field. They announced before the play exactly where they were going to run the ball. Opponents *still* could not stop them. The third-to-last game of the season, though, was against West Point Academy. If any team could stop the Indians, it was the Army men.

The Final Games

The game against West Point on November 9, 1912, felt bigger than just a football game to the Carlisle players. It felt like a chance to avenge some of history's past wrongs—in particular the wars between the Indians and the United States Army. In fact, the Battle of Wounded Knee, which was the last major battle in the Indian Wars, had occurred just twenty-two years earlier.

Although Jim was a great athlete, he had conflicting feelings about being in the spotlight and all the pressure to succeed that fell on his shoulders.

West Point

The United States Military Academy is located in West Point, New York, along the Hudson River. It was founded in 1802 by Thomas Jefferson to train officers for the U.S. Army. (The school began admitting women in 1976.) The school is the oldest military academy in the United States. West Point, as it is known, is a four-year college. Its students, known as cadets, study normal courses in literature, math, and science, but also take classes in military history, strategy, and leadership. They also take part in a full range of athletics. Some of the male students play football. Graduates become second lieutenants in the U.S. Army and normally must serve six years following graduation. At one time, the Army football team was the best in the nation.

Shown here, cadets from the United States Military Academy participate in the Inaugural Parade for President Barack Obama on January 20, 2009.

The Army had a strong football team in Jim Thorpe's time. In this c. 1916 photograph, the Army is playing against the Navy at the Polo Grounds in New York.

(Carlisle had only played Army once before, in 1905, and won an exceptionally rough and bloody game, 6–5.)

"[Coach] Warner had no trouble getting the boys keyed up for that game," Gus Welch, the quarterback of the team, said in later years. "He reminded the boys that it was the fathers and grandfathers of these Army players who fought the Indians. That was enough."

The battle on the field rested on the shoulders of the two teams' best players: halfback Thorpe for Carlisle and halfback Dwight David Eisenhower, the future U.S. president, for Army. Each team would depend on its star to succeed.

The score remained close at halftime, with Carlisle ahead 7–6. But in the second half, the Indians took total control of

Mighty Dwight

Dwight David Eisenhower was the thirty-fourth president of the United States (1953–1961). Before he became president, he was a standout athlete, and a five-star general in the army.

Eisenhower, known as "Ike," entered the U.S. Military Academy in 1911 and made the varsity football team in 1912. During that season, he faced off against the Carlisle Indians and Jim Thorpe. Although the game received a lot of attention, the Indians easily won 27–6. "[Thorpe] was able to do everything that anyone else could, but he could do it better," Eisenhower said about Jim.

Ike hurt his knee the game following the Carlisle matchup that season, and he never played football again. Eisenhower graduated from the academy in 1915 and trained tank crews in World War I. He moved up the ranks, however, and in World War II, Eisenhower became the Supreme Allied Commander in Europe. He planned the **D-Day** invasion of France in 1944. He became enormously popular, and people convinced him to run for president. As president, Eisenhower ended the Korean War, launched the space program, and presided over an era of economic prosperity.

Before becoming president of the United States in 1953, former Army football star Dwight Eisenhower was a five-star general. In this famous photo, he instructs paratroopers during World War II.

the game. Eisenhower collided with a teammate and sat out most of the second half. Thorpe, though, was nothing short of spectacular. He averaged running 10 yards per carry and set up all of Carlisle's touchdowns. The final score was 27–6. The stories in the paper the next day fawned over the Indians, especially Thorpe. "He simply ran wild," one *New York Times* story said about Jim, "while the Cadets tried in vain to stop his progress. It was like trying to clutch a shadow."

Jim and his teammates were overjoyed with the victory. Unfortunately, the celebration didn't last too long. The following week, the team played overconfidently and lost 34–26 to Penn. Carlisle rebounded with wins over the Springfield Training School (30–24) and Brown University (32–0) for the last games of the season. In the Brown game, Thorpe scored three touchdowns and kicked two field goals. Because of the loss to Penn, Carlisle's chance to be crowned national champions was over. The Indians still finished the season with a spectacular 12–1–1 record, and they outscored their opponents 504–114. Thorpe scored 198 of those points for an average of 14 per game! He was named a first-team All-America for the second year in a row. Newspaper writers continued to pile on the praise to Thorpe and his athletic skills. Coach Warner summed it up best by saying, "Thorpe is the most marvelous all-around athlete that the world has ever seen."

CHAPTER 8

Scandal

I was not wise in the ways of the world and did not realize this was wrong.

About two months after Carlisle's 1912 football season ended, a story broke that changed Thorpe's life. The headline of the story in the *Worcester Telegram* read THORPE WITH PROFESSIONAL BASEBALL TEAM.

The article was referring to the summers of 1909 and 1910, when Jim had played semiprofessional baseball in North Carolina. During these summers, Jim had been paid a small sum of money to play in the East Carolina League. Why was this a big deal? According to Olympic rules, athletes had to be amateurs, or unpaid athletes, in order to compete in the Games. Professionals, or paid athletes, were not allowed—even if they were paid to play a sport other than the one they competed in at the Olympics. Jim had violated these rules when he won the gold medals at the 1912 Games.

Roy Johnson, the writer for the *Worcester Telegram*, had first caught wind of this story two months earlier, during Carlisle's football season. It was a week before the Indians' final game against Brown, and the team was practicing in Worcester, Massachusetts (about forty miles from Brown). Locals, as well as the press, came to watch the team play. Johnson was standing next to Charles Clancy, a minor-league baseball manager who now lived in the area but had spent time coaching in the Carolina league. When Thorpe jogged by, Clancy mentioned to Johnson that he knew Thorpe from the semipro league. "Yes," Clancy told the *Telegram* reporter, "Thorpe had been paid to play."

Johnson could not believe the scoop he'd just landed: Thorpe wasn't an amateur when he competed in the Olympics. He never should have been allowed to go for gold! Johnson spent the next couple of months researching this lead and making sure his facts were accurate. The story was finally printed in the paper on January 22, 1913. The consequences were immediate.

Returning the Medals

After the piece ran in the *Telegram*, other newspapers picked up the story as well. On January 28, a headline in the *New York Times* read OLYMPIC PRIZES LOST, THORPE NO AMATEUR. The article stated that Thorpe had confessed in a letter to James Sullivan, the chairman of the Amateur Athletic Union (AAU), that he had indeed played professional baseball during those summers. "I was not wise in the ways of the world and did not realize this was wrong," Jim confessed in the letter.

Sullivan, whose organization selected the U.S. Olympic Team, felt he had no other choice but to follow the rules he helped create: Jim had to forfeit, or give up, his Olympic medals. "Thorpe's case is at once

This is a gold medal from the 2008 Olympic Games in Beijing. Jim Thorpe won two such medals at the 1912 Games, but had to return them because he had earlier been paid to play baseball.

one of the greatest tragedies and marvels of amateur athletics," Sullivan later commented.

Jim was devastated, and seemingly confused by why the news that he had played professional baseball was such a big deal. "What's two months of baseball got to do with all the jumping and running and field work I did in Stockholm?" Thorpe asked his coach, Pop Warner. "I never got paid for any of that, did I?"

"Thorpe's case is at once one of the greatest tragedies and marvels of amateur athletics," . . .

In fact, the general public shared this opinion as well. Columns ran in newspapers across the country supporting Thorpe. The whole world seemed to be on Jim's side.

GREAT BRITAIN THINKS NONE THE WORSE OF THE INDIAN FOR HIS BASEBALL CRIME, ran a headline in the *London Daily News.* Another headline in the *Toronto Mail* read CANADIANS STAND FIRM WITH OUR JIM THORPE.

Along with the worldwide support of Thorpe, there was also much disapproval of Pop Warner and James Sullivan for letting Jim take all the blame. Both men, critics suspected, knew Jim had been paid to play ball but did not want to confess this was the case. Pop, who secretly paid his own football players at Carlisle, did not want anybody probing into his own athletic program.

If Sullivan admitted he had known Jim played pro ball, his whole stand on amateur athleticism would ring false. After all, Sullivan was one of the founders and the president of the AAU—an organization based on the belief that athletes play sports for the love of competition, not for the money.

Thus, it was Pop, after consulting with Sullivan, who encouraged Jim to write the confession in the first place. Jim

Pop Warner, shown here on a train in 1934 late in his long coaching career, encouraged Jim to write a confession—but the coach's motives were suspect.

looked up to his coach and relied heavily on his advice. He would do most anything Warner told him to—even if it meant lying.

Pop helped Jim write the draft. In the letter, under Pop's advice, Thorpe falsely stated: "I never told anybody at school about [my ball playing] until today."

Pop helped Jim box up his medals and send them back to Sweden. Hugo Wieslander of Sweden, the silver medal winner in the decathlon, was bumped up to first, and Ferdinand Bie of Norway, the silver medal winner in the pentathlon, was awarded the gold. Jim became the first athlete in history to have his name banished from the Olympic record books for professionalism. Supporters tried to raise money to replace the medals, but

Paying Players at Carlisle

Pop Warner's refusal to say that he knew Thorpe was paid to play baseball was ridiculous. Pop and Jim were undeniably close. As one suspicious writer put it, "Could Thorpe have left Carlisle for two full years and Warner not have known where he had been?"

In fact, Pop paid his own players to play football—a clear violation of the rules of amateur athletics. At the time Pop coached at Carlisle, the only team-sport athletes considered professional were baseball players.

Carlisle players received "loans" during every season. Some of the star players were even given a charge account at a clothing store in downtown Carlisle. If a player drank too much at a bar and got too rowdy or got into a fight, Warner paid police officers to bring the athlete home and keep the event quiet. W. G. Thompson, the first football coach at Carlisle, was a critic of Warner's loose policies and was a source for a story that appeared in the *Chicago Sunday Tribune* in 1907. The headline of the story was CARLISLE'S ATHLETIC POLICY CRITICIZED. Thompson alleged that every one of Warner's players was paid *something* by the end of the season.

Thompson maintained that Warner kept a list of prices for accomplishments on the field, delivering different amounts of money for such things as touchdowns and blocked kicks. "This was in violation of the ethics of college sport and made the players professionals," Thompson said.

Warner also took money for himself. He used athletic association funds to build himself a house, as well as to pay bills.

Despite all these wrongdoings, Warner's programs flourished. By the time he resigned from Carlisle in 1915, he had won 78 of the 100 games he coached.

Thorpe told them to give the money to charity instead. "I didn't have too much," Jim told a friend, "and now I don't have the medals."

Looking toward the Future

Jim did not spend much time dwelling on his lost medals. He had his future to consider. He realized if he wasn't allowed to compete as an amateur anymore, he needed to decide on a pro career. And just as when he had come back from Stockholm, offers came pouring in from entertainment agents hoping Jim would become a movie star, boxing managers wanting him to take up boxing, and major-league baseball teams trying to enlist him. Jim decided he wanted to play baseball.

Despite never having proved himself on the baseball field, Jim got interest from six major-league baseball teams that made Jim offers to play for their clubs. Team owners thought that even if Jim turned out not to be a good player, he would still generate ticket sales

After Jim decided to play professional baseball, he quickly drew interest from several major-league clubs. This photograph shows Jim swinging a bat at the Polo Grounds, the home of the New York Giants.

because of his fame. In the end, Thorpe decided to go with the highest bidder.

On February 1, 1913, Jim, wearing a purple hat and a tailored blue suit, signed a three-year deal with the New York Giants for $6,000 a year, with a $500 signing bonus. It was the most ever paid to a major-league rookie. The Giants' manager, John McGraw, admitted that he had never seen Thorpe play, and didn't even know if he hit right- or left-handed. (Thorpe was a

Before John McGraw became a manager, he was one of the best players of his time. In this photograph from the 1900s, McGraw plays for the New York Giants.

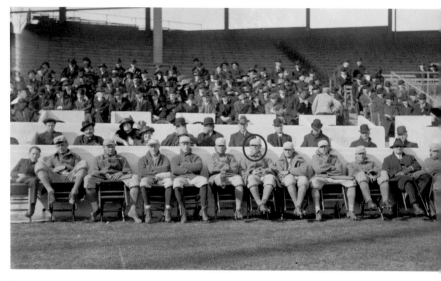

Jim (circled) was among the Giants' rookies who posed for this photo at the Polo Grounds in 1913.

righty.) "If he can only hit in batting practice, the fans that will pay to see him will more than make up for his salary," McGraw told a friend after the signing.

In his own mind, though, Jim wasn't playing to bring in money for the ball club. He wanted to make a real go at being a pro—and being a good one at that. "It has been my ambition to become a big-time ball player since my school days," Thorpe told reporters on signing day. "And now I have a chance to have the ambition of my life realized."

CHAPTER 9

Life as a Pro

*One day, I hit three home runs into three
different states.*

Thorpe's first season as a pro baseball player was a
difficult one. Although Jim was the most natural of
athletes, he had never had any formal baseball training.
While attending the Giants' training camp in Texas,
Thorpe was noticeably less skilled, especially when
batting, than most of his teammates. While at bat, he
had trouble recognizing the pitches. "I can't seem to hit
curveballs," Jim admitted.

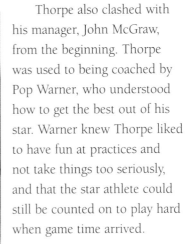

Thorpe also clashed with
his manager, John McGraw,
from the beginning. Thorpe
was used to being coached by
Pop Warner, who understood
how to get the best out of his
star. Warner knew Thorpe liked
to have fun at practices and
not take things too seriously,
and that the star athlete could
still be counted on to play hard
when game time arrived.

Jim is shown working out with the Giants
in this photo. His first season with New
York was a difficult one.

One of Baseball's Best

John McGraw (1873–1934) was one of the most successful baseball managers in the history of the game. He led the New York Giants to eleven National League pennants, or championships, and three World Series titles in twenty-seven full seasons, plus parts of four others (1902–1932). As a manager, he won an astonishing 2,784 games—the second most of all time.

McGraw also helped develop a strategy of the game called "inside baseball." He emphasized strategy over pure power, and used pinch runners and pinch hitters, or substitute runners and hitters, far more than any other manager at the time.

Although McGraw was an amazing manager, he also had a well-earned reputation as a hothead. His temper was not reserved just for Jim Thorpe, but released upon anybody and everybody around him. He was ejected from 131 games during his career—a record that stood for seventy-five years. A third baseman for the 1909 Giants, Arlie Latham, described him this way: "McGraw eats gunpowder every morning for breakfast and washes it down with warm blood."

Although he last managed in 1932, the Giants' John McGraw still ranks second on baseball's all-time list for wins.

McGraw, on the other hand, never understood Thorpe's sense of humor or playfulness. Jim enjoyed roughhousing with his Giant teammates. In fact, he tried to take on three or even four teammates at a time in wrestling matches. When McGraw got word of this behavior, he threatened Jim with a 100-dollar fine if he caught him "fighting" again.

According to reports from teammates, at times McGraw tried to control Thorpe by calling him racist names and taunting him. All this tactic did was make Jim more likely to misbehave, and less willing to work hard for his coach.

As a result, Thorpe spent much of his rookie season on the bench—and hating it. He played in just 19 of 156 games, mostly as a pinch hitter and pinch runner, and had just 5 hits in 35 at bats. "I felt like a sitting hen, not a ball player," said Thorpe about the first season.

Most likely, Jim was thankful when his rookie season finally ended. After all, he had something to look forward to—his wedding to his Carlisle sweetheart, Ivy Miller.

Life with Ivy

Thorpe had stayed in touch with his first love, Iva "Ivy" Miller, after she graduated from Carlisle in 1912. Ivy's relatives, as well as Pop Warner, had warned her against Thorpe. They thought he was too unreliable for the smart and hardworking young girl. But Ivy was strong-willed and defiant, just like Jim. Over the years, they had carried on a secret romance. Thorpe wrote Ivy love letters while away at the Olympics. In turn, she had her own nickname for him—"Snooks." Finally, after Jim's rookie season ended, Ivy's relatives relented and granted her permission to marry Jim.

The wedding took place on October 14, 1913, at Saint

Patrick's Church in the town of Carlisle. All of the couple's parents were deceased, so Carlisle superintendent Moses Friedman gave away the bride and hosted the reception in his home. Movie companies filmed the ceremony, and it was shown in theaters across the country. The local paper described the bride as a "laughing, dark-eyed princess."

Finally, after Jim's rookie season ended, Ivy's relatives relented and granted her permission to marry Jim.

The weekend after the wedding, the young couple embarked on an all-expense-paid honeymoon that took them all over the world. It was part of a good-will tour by the Giants and the Chicago White Sox. The two teams played exhibition games in sixteen states and fourteen countries, including Great Britain, Italy, France, Egypt, and Japan. Although the trip's focus was on baseball, Ivy would remember some fond times just with Jim. "We danced on deck," she wrote in her diary of one long boat trip. "Snooks taught me some new tango steps."

When the newlyweds arrived back in New York in the spring of 1914, they settled in an apartment near the Polo Grounds in Upper Manhattan, where the Giants played. Although Jim's next two seasons weren't much more successful than his first—he had a combined 18 hits in 83 at bats—one highlight of the 1914 season always stood out to him. "One day, I hit three home runs into three different states," Jim revealed.

The three blasts occurred during the Giants' spring training, when they were playing in a part of the country that is formed by Texas, Arkansas, and Oklahoma. Jim hit one ball over the right-field fence, which was in Oklahoma, one ball over the left-field fence, which was in Arkansas, and one over the center-field fence, which was in Texas.

The following spring after the "triple-homer game," Jim experienced an even more remarkable event: on May 8, 1915, Thorpe's wife gave birth to a son, James Francis, Jr. Jim grew to love his son more than he loved anyone else in the world.

Tragedy Strikes

After the baseball season ended in the fall of 1915, Jim accepted an opportunity to play his once-favorite sport, football, and get paid for it. In truth, Jim may have become involved with football again because of his son. Despite making a healthy salary playing baseball, Jim couldn't help but think the more money he made, the more he could provide for his growing family.

During baseball's off-season, Jim worked as an assistant football coach at the University of Indiana, specializing in teaching the players how to kick. Jim also earned a small amount of money playing football for the Pine Village Athletic Club in Indiana. (There was no national pro football league at the time. A few clubs paid former college players, as well as current college players who competed under false names, small sums of money to compete.

Attendance swelled at Canton Bulldogs' games after Jim joined the pro football team in 1915.

The teams played other local clubs in their area.) While in Indiana, Jim was approached by a former Carlisle teammate, Bill Gardner. Gardner played for another "pro football team," the Canton Bulldogs in Canton, Ohio. Gardner asked Jim if he wanted to join the Bulldogs as well. The team manager, Jack Cusack, said he would pay Thorpe $250 per game—a hefty sum of money in those days. The Bulldogs' chief competitor was the Massillon Tigers, a club just ten miles away. The rivalry had become intense, and Cusack was willing to pay big bucks to ensure a victory. Jim agreed to play for them.

Although no stats were kept at the time, Jim's presence made a big impact on the team's popularity. Before Jim's arrival, Canton averaged about 1,500 paid fans per game. After Jim joined the team, the crowd size swelled to more than 6,000. Ticket prices

Jim (upright on the left) moves in to make a tackle on this play for the Canton Bulldogs against the Columbus Panhandles in 1915.

also increased—from 50 to 75 cents. And, although Canton didn't beat Massillon in the first game they played with Thorpe, the Bulldogs did win the next meeting between the clubs. Canton manager Jack Cusack had this to say about Thorpe: "Throughout Jim's first two years with the Bulldogs, he had consistently outstanding games. His tremendous power up the middle and his **broken-field running** [was] the greatest the spectators had ever witnessed. No one was Jim's equal on the [football field]."

However, Thorpe wasn't receiving the same praise for his play on the baseball diamond—where he was supposed to be playing as the "real" professional. In fact, he didn't even play in a major-league game in 1916. Instead, he was sent down to a minor-league team in Milwaukee, Wisconsin, for the year.

In the 1917 season, the Giants loaned Jim to major-league team the Cincinnati Reds, where he was at least given playing time. In 77 games in Ohio, Jim had a .247 batting average in 251 appearances at the plate. He was called back to the Giants on August 1 and played the remaining 26 games in New York, where his batting average dropped to .193 over 57 at bats. He did

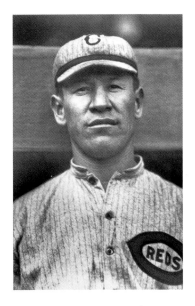

Jim is pictured while on loan to the Cincinnati Reds in 1917. He got a chance to play regularly in about half a season with the Reds, but most of his big-league career was spent on the bench with the New York Giants.

get to appear in the World Series for one game—a first for any former Olympic athlete. The 1918 season proved to be more of the same. Jim batted .248 in 113 at bats.

Stats aside, something far more important than baseball soon took Thorpe's attention and heart away from the game. His son, Jim Jr., died at age three in late September of 1918. Most reports say he died of influenza, a serious flu virus. The entire country was seized by this epidemic. All told, some 675,000 Americans would eventually die from this particular virus. Although Jim had experienced tragic losses before with the deaths of his brother, mother, and father, losing his son proved hardest of all.

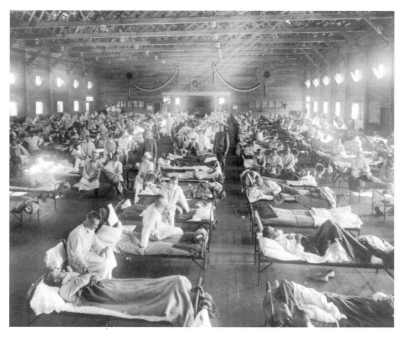

The flu epidemic of 1918 killed more than 50 million people worldwide, including Jim Thorpe, Jr. This photograph shows an emergency hospital at Camp Funston in Kansas.

The Deadly Flu

Today when somebody gets the flu, it usually means a runny nose, a bad cough, or an upset stomach. Most of the time, the person is healthy again within a couple of days. In 1918, though, the flu was more than a common cold: it was a deadly virus.

The influenza virus of 1918, the one that killed Jim Thorpe's son, Jim Jr., was one of the most serious epidemics ever. From March 1918 to June 1920, the contagious virus spread around the world. A flu-stricken patient had trouble breathing because his or her lungs became backed up with mucus. When the virus got really bad, the sick person coughed up blood. All told, the virus killed 50 million people worldwide. A famous child's rhyme came about from this sad time. It went:

I had a little bird
Its name was Enza
I opened the window
And in-flu-enza.

This makeshift courtroom in San Francisco was set up in a park during the flu epidemic of 1918 to keep the virus from spreading indoors.

Ivy called little Jim's death the tragedy of her husband's life. "He was heartbroken when that boy died," she said.

Jim's final major-league baseball season was in 1919. Devastated by his son's death, Jim became an unreliable player. He was late, or skipped practices altogether. He also started to drink more and more. Although McGraw tried to be sympathetic, he couldn't tolerate Thorpe's lack of commitment to his team. There was constant tension between the two men. The relationship soon came to an explosive ending. According to Giant teammate Al Schacht, McGraw called Jim a "dumb Indian" after Thorpe missed a signal while running the bases. The insult was more than Jim could stand. He chased his coach around the field, intent on beating him up. Thorpe's teammates chased him down and held him back. Soon after the incident, Thorpe was sent to the Boston Braves. He played the remainder of the season in Massachusetts (averaging a career best .327 in 60 games).

After the 1919 season ended, Jim never played in the majors again. He played mostly with Triple-A (the highest level) minor-league teams, lasting until 1928. But his real focus for the next nine years would be not on baseball, but on his pro football career.

CHAPTER 10

The Beginning and the End

One must quit sometime.

The date was August 20, 1920, and sports history was about to be made. The state of "pro" football had become messy. Players jumped from club team to club team, depending which team offered the most money. More and more college players competed illegally under false names. Team owners decided a pro league should be formed, like major-league baseball, where all teams had to follow the same rules. Representatives from the Akron Pros, the Canton Bulldogs, the Cleveland Indians, and the Dayton Triangles all met in an automobile showroom in Canton, Ohio. The end result: the formation of the American Professional Football Conference—which would eventually become today's National Football League (NFL).

At a second meeting, held on September 17 in Canton, additional teams were added and the league name was changed to the American Professional Football Association (APFA). But, more importantly, Jim Thorpe was named president. The league wanted to capitalize on, or take advantage of, Thorpe's famous name. The owners thought he would bring respectability to the young league.

Jim was paid a yearly salary of $2,500 to act as president (about $80,000 by today's standards), but in

Jim was still an active player when he was named the first president of the National Football League (then called the American Professional Football Association) in 1920. This 1921 photograph shows Jim in his football uniform.

truth he had no real responsibility and only lasted one season in the job. He was simply needed to be the "face" of the league as it tried to get off the ground. In many ways, this was typical of the treatment Thorpe had received throughout his life: other people exploiting, or selfishly using, his talents to gain something for themselves. In this case, the new football league needed Jim's famous name to generate ticket sales and promote the league around the country.

Although Jim was aware he was being used for his famous name, he was not upset about this. In fact, he simply enjoyed the large salary he was paid. Jim's heart was never in administrative work, though; he just wanted to be a player on the field.

Even as the league president, Jim did continue to play for the Canton Bulldogs in the 1920 season. During warm-ups, Thorpe showed off his kicking ability. He placed balls at midfield and alternated kicking them between the goalposts at either end. Although there were no modern statistics kept during games, opponents and teammates marveled at Thorpe's play. "You'd dive at him and hit him and after time, when you came to, you'd wonder if the roof had fallen in," said Carp Julian, one of Thorpe's Canton teammates. "He was like an oak tree doing a hundred yards in ten seconds."

"You'd dive at him and hit him and after time, when you came to, you'd wonder if the roof had fallen in," . . .

All-Indian Team

Jim played his second season in the APFA with Cleveland. In the third season (the first in which the league was known as the NFL), Jim returned to his roots: he was named coach, as well as a player, on a team called the Oorang Indians, which was made up entirely of Native American players. The team was financially backed by Walter Lingo, owner of the Oorang Dog Kennels in the small town of La Rue, Ohio. The real purpose of the team wasn't to win football games, but instead to provide advertisement for Lingo's Airedale terriers, a type of hunting dog. (Lingo sold his dogs through a hunting and trapping magazine.) The dogs, as well as the Indians, provided the

The NFL's Oorang team in 1922 was made up entirely of Native Americans. Jim (standing in the middle of the back row) was Oorang's coach and star, but the team didn't win many games.

crowds with pregame and halftime entertainment. There were shooting exhibitions, in which the dogs retrieved the targets, and traditional Indian dances and knife-throwing demonstrations. Stories even reported a player wrestling a bear on occasion!

Although the players on the team knew this entertainment could seem silly, they were still happy to be paid to play. Many of the players had been teammates back at the Carlisle School, and they all enjoyed being together again.

The team was also a wild and rowdy bunch off the field. Officially, Jim was the coach, but he much preferred just being "one of the boys." The squad played all its games on the road because Lingo wanted to reach as many potential customers as possible. In bars across the country, Jim and his teammates stayed out until early morning. There were many reports of late-night brawls and encounters with the local police.

Unfortunately, the Indians weren't nearly as entertaining on the playing field. In 1922 and 1923, they came away with a combined three victories. Toward the end of the 1923 season, the novelty of the team ended, and fans stopped showing up to games. Lingo pulled his financial backing, and the team folded. Despite the abrupt ending, Jim still remembered this team as a wonderful bunch. "My professional football career reached its climax when I assembled the greatest Indian team of all time," he recalled. "The Oorang Indians: one of the finest groups of professionals that ever played together."

During the years Jim had played for the Indians, though, his personal life had taken a turn for the worst. Though he and Ivy had been blessed with three more children—all daughters: Gail, Charlotte, and Grace—Jim was rarely home. He stayed out too late and drank too much. Just as he did during his days in boarding school, Jim became restless if he stayed in one place for too long. Although he loved his children dearly, the day-to-day responsibility of parenthood was too much for Jim to handle. He preferred to be free and on the road. As his daughters got older, they learned to accept their father for who he was, and not judge him for being away so much. Charlotte had this to say about him: "Dad did not try to set himself up for others to follow. Young and old loved him for what he was, a big, warm, fun-loving boy-man."

In 1923, Jim and Ivy divorced after ten years of marriage. In October of 1925, Jim, age thirty-eight, married Freeda Kirkpatrick, age seventeen. When Jim and Freeda first met,

In this c. 1931 photograph, Jim visits with his daughter Grace at the Haskell Institute—the same school he once attended.

she was a high school student in La Rue, Ohio; eventually she worked as a secretary for the Oorang Kennel Company. Love letters written to Freeda around this time reveal just how happy she made him. But Jim's second marriage was also the beginning of an unhappy time and a slow end to his athletic career.

Hanging Up the Cleats

Jim played professional football through the 1926 season. He didn't play football at all in 1927. (Sources later revealed that Thorpe was playing on a Native-American all-star basketball

Basketball, Too?

In 2005, a book collector named Anthony Barone, Jr., bought a book for six dollars titled *Jesse James and His Greatest Hauls*. The book, written in the 1920s, was about the adventures of the infamous train robber Jesse James. Tucked inside the pages, Barone discovered a big red ticket, six inches long. The ticket was for an exhibition basketball game played on March 1, 1927, and featured Jim Thorpe and "His World Famous Indians."

"A ticket is a fabulous, beautiful find," said Bob Wheeler, who wrote a book on Thorpe. "It's a rare, small thing that can tell us about bigger things."

Prior to Barone's finding this ticket, most historians, as well as Thorpe's family, never even knew Jim played hoops as an adult. But after this discovery, experts did even more digging. They found out that Thorpe and fellow Native Americans played on a 45-game tour, in parts of New York, Pennsylvania, and Ohio, in 1927.

Unfortunately, stats don't exist from these games, and it is unknown just how good a player Thorpe was. But one thing is for sure—the team drew crowds wherever it went. Newspaper articles that appeared at the time included reports of sold-out gymnasiums. "[Basketball] is another whole area of sport that Thorpe excelled at," said Bill Crawford, who also wrote a book on Jim. "It shows another side of his athleticism."

team at this time.) In 1928, he played one football game for the Chicago Cardinals on Thanksgiving. After that, he never set foot on the field as a pro again.

Though he was playing at the highest level, the last five years of Thorpe's football career were more sad than memorable. He bounced from team to team, playing for the Rock Island (Illinois) Independents, the New York Giants, the Canton Bulldogs, and in his final season, the one appearance for the Cardinals. Thorpe was noticeably slower by then, and was primarily a punter and kicker. The fact that he had lost a step, perhaps a couple, was clear in an exhibition game following the 1925 season.

During this time, the Chicago Bears were on a 67-game postseason tour across the country. They had just signed a halfback named Harold "Red" Grange, and they wanted to show him off. Grange had been an All-America at the University of Illinois. The owners of the NFL hoped Grange would become the new face of the league.

Former college star Red Grange's signing with the Chicago Bears in 1925 often is credited with putting the NFL on the national sports map.

Red Grange (1903–1991)

While Jim Thorpe grabbed public attention for football in the early 1910s, the 1920s belonged to Red Grange. Nicknamed "the Galloping Ghost" as a star player with the University of Illinois because he was so tough to tackle, Grange quickly became the nation's top football player. After leaving Illinois, he set up his own team. With Grange in the lineup, fans filled stadiums. Working with a promoter named C. C. Pyle, Grange made a lot of money playing what were basically exhibition games in New York, Chicago, and other places. The young NFL finally convinced him to join, and many call his signing the biggest thing to happen to pro football for decades. He only played in the NFL for eight years (1925, 1927, and 1929–1934) and his stats pale in comparison to those of today's stars. But the power of Red's running and his amazing celebrity (he even starred in movies of his life) made him one of football's all-time heroes.

Red Grange worked with promoter C. C. Pyle (left) to travel around the country playing exhibition football games.

Thorpe joined several of his Rock Island teammates to play in an exhibition game against Grange and the Bears in Florida. The game was billed as a clash between the "rising star and the aging legend." Thorpe wrote in a letter to his wife Freeda, dated December 27, 1925: "I am going to show that Red Grange has nothing on me in the line of football." Unfortunately, this was not the case. Grange had the better day—running for a 70-yard touchdown as the Bears won 17–3. Grange said after the game that he thought Thorpe seemed slow and out of shape. He even commented that Jim fumbled, or dropped the ball, several times. "I never saw him in his prime," Red said later on.

Thorpe and his teammates stayed in Florida through January of 1926. There, they played exhibition games against club and independent teams. Newspaper stories of the day covered these games in a fun and upbeat manner. Jim felt otherwise—as revealed in a letter to his wife dated January 14, 1926: "I guess I should never look for the best as things have sure gone wrong."

A day after this letter was written, on January 15, 1926, Thorpe, just shy of forty, announced his retirement. "One must quit sometime," Thorpe told the *New York Times*. "My earning days in athletics are at an end, and while sports have been my livelihood, I have really played for the love of competition: I have a yearning to hunt and fish back with my people."

Jim did end up playing one more season for the Canton Bulldogs, and one last game for Chicago. But, his feelings remained true and he finally did call it quits for good.

CHAPTER 11

Life After Sports

I can't decide if I was well named or not. For many times the path has gleamed bright for me—but just as often it has been dark and bitter.

After Jim's athletic career ended, he felt lost. He didn't know what to do with himself without sports, nor did he know how to support his ever-growing family. In addition to his three daughters from his first marriage to Ivy, he eventually had four more sons with Freeda—Carl Phillip, William, Richard, and John (Jack). What made Jim's search for a productive life even tougher was that it was the beginning of the Great Depression. The Depression, which officially began in October of 1929, was a worldwide economic downturn that left millions of people penniless, jobless, and in some cases, homeless.

Jim and his family had been living in Oklahoma. But he soon decided to take his family farther west—to Hollywood, California.

Jim has fun playing with his boys in California in the early 1930s. In this photo, Phillip (left) is 4 years old and William is 3.

The Great Depression

October 29, 1929, will forever be known as "Black Tuesday." This was the day the stock market crashed. Historians point to this date as the onset of the Great Depression.

Many people lost all their savings. Worse than that, banks also lost a lot of money that day. By 1932, the United States banking system had collapsed and 12.5 million Americans were unemployed. People could barely feed themselves—malnutrition was a serious problem.

In 1932, Franklin Delano Roosevelt was elected president of the United States. He introduced the "New Deal," a series of economic reforms to help the American people. Roosevelt helped restructure the banking system, create new jobs, and build new roads, schools, and parks.

The New Deal gave millions of Americans hope, even if it didn't immediately reverse the Depression. Many historians note that World War II (which the United States entered after the attack on Pearl Harbor on December 7, 1941) played the crucial role in lifting the United States out of the Depression. As a result of U.S. involvement in the war, new machinery, such as airplanes and bombs, had to be made. This helped create many new jobs and gave people a renewed sense of purpose.

Americans did not have enough food to eat during the Great Depression. This is a bread line in New York in the early 1930s.

Jim started a movie career in Hollywood after moving to California. He often played Native American roles.

He wanted to become a movie star. Soon after he arrived, Metro-Goldwyn Studios bought the rights to his life story, in order to make a film about him. Jim, never good with money, sold the rights for a mere $1,500, far below what he should have been paid. Worse still, the proposed MGM film, named *Red Son of Carlisle*, was never made because of continuing disagreements over who legally owned the story.

In January of 1930, Jim landed a job as master of ceremonies for a footrace across the country called the "Bunion Derby." The race, organized by C. C. Pyle, a theater owner and sports agent, was run from the East Coast to the West Coast over the course of a couple months. (The previous year, 199 runners went from Los

Angeles, California, to New York City in the first Bunion Derby.)
Unfortunately, C. C. Pyle could not turn a profit on the second
race. He was not able to pay the winner, John Salo, the promised
$25,000 prize money. Thorpe, who expected $50 for his part
of being on hand to help start the race and lending his famous
name to publicize the event, had to sue Pyle to get paid.

Thorpe did eventually land some small roles in Hollywood
films—mostly uncredited ones as a Native American. His first
was in a 1931 film called *Battling with Buffalo Bill.* Thorpe played
an Indian named Swift Arrow. Jim also took small jobs on the
side when he wasn't acting. He even worked as a digger for
the building of a new Los Angeles County Hospital. His pay
was a pitiful 50 cents an hour. In the summer of 1932, the
Olympics were held in Los Angeles. Thorpe, perhaps the most
amazing Olympian ever, didn't even have enough money to buy
a ticket for the Games. When word of this reached the press,
stories were written about Thorpe's sad financial state. Charles
Curtis, the vice president of the United States at the time and an

American Indian, declared,
"Jim Thorpe will sit with
me." When Jim took his
seat next to Curtis at the
beginning of the Games, the
crowd of 105,000 people
gave the former star a
standing ovation. Jim was

One of the jobs Jim took in
California was digging ditches on
the construction site for a new
hospital in Los Angeles.

touched by the crowd's cheering and was thankful that Curtis had offered him the ticket. Thorpe did not feel sorry for himself. He was proud of his accomplishments and proud of himself, despite having fallen on hard times.

After the Olympics ended, Jim went back to work, appearing in films such as the original *King Kong* (as a "native dancer") and other movies titled *Sweepings* ("Indian") and *Behold My Wife* ("Indian Chief"). Jim also traveled the country making speeches to promote athletics and sportsmanship at schools and charity events. He often appeared at these places for free, while struggling even to pay his own traveling costs. On December 6, 1934, Jim spoke at Long Beach (California) Polytechnic High School. In his remarks he noted, "Athletics give you a fighting spirit to battle your problems of life, they build sportsmanship."

> *"Athletics give you a fighting spirit to battle your problems of life, they build sportsmanship."*

Unfortunately for Thorpe, he had plenty of problems—too little money to support his growing family, a struggle with alcoholism—to battle.

Back to Oklahoma

In 1937, Thorpe decided to take his family back to Oklahoma. Although he continued to travel back and forth to California to act, he also wanted to become more involved in Native American politics. As Jim had gotten older, his interest in his people's affairs had grown. He now understood how unfairly Native Americans had been treated in the past. He wanted to help right some of the wrongs. Indians had been granted citizenship in 1924. But the Bureau of Indian Affairs, a government organization that had been started in 1824, still played an active

Jim never forgot his Native American roots. He became increasingly involved in political causes important to Native Americans.

role in Native American lives. The bureau managed the Indians' businesses, provided services, and meddled in land disputes. Thorpe thought the organization should be abolished, although it is actually still in existence today. "We are trying to keep our tribe free from government meddling," Thorpe was quoted as saying in the *New York Times* on December 12, 1937. "To give the Indian a chance to stand on his own."

Jim also began lecturing more and more. A charitable organization called the Circus Saints and Sinners financed Jim to go on a countrywide lecture tour. He gave inspirational talks on his career, sports, and Indian culture and tradition. He even dressed in traditional Indian clothing and headdress. At the end of his speeches, Thorpe would remind his audience: "I would like to ask every one of you here to work for the improvement of Indian conditions. They can be bettered with your help."

. . . Thorpe would remind his audience: "I would like to ask every one of you here to work for the improvement of Indian conditions. They can be bettered with your help."

With Thorpe rarely at home—and when he was, he was addicted to drinking too much just as he was on the road—his wife, Freeda, was left alone to raise their four boys, who were three to thirteen years old. Freeda finally decided the relationship had to end. On April 4, 1941, after fifteen years of marriage, she filed for divorce.

According to Charlotte, one of Thorpe's daughters from his first marriage, Jim was depressed and disappointed by Freeda's decision. Charlotte said that during this sad time, her father came to visit her in Chicago where she lived. He had this to say about his Native American name, Wa-Tho-Huck, or Bright Path: "I can't decide if I was well named or not. For many times the path has gleamed bright for me—but just as often it has been dark and bitter."

The United States had entered World War II in December 1941. With the war now in full swing, Thorpe wanted to help fight. But he was now in his mid-fifties and considered too old to

Jim helped the war effort by working in security for a Michigan factory that made bomber airplanes. He is shown checking an employee's pass before permitting him to enter the plant.

serve. He decided to help the war effort in another way. In March of 1942, he traveled to Dearborn, Michigan, where he worked in security at Ford's River Rouge Plant. The plant had been built to produce B-24 Liberator Bombers, airplanes that dropped bombs for the war.

Just eleven months later, Thorpe suffered a heart attack. While in the hospital, he received hundreds of letters from fans, mostly teenagers, wishing him a speedy recovery. One letter in particular, from a boy in North Carolina, was a favorite of Jim's. "If you get well," the boy wrote, "sports will mean more to me and millions of other American boys like me. To know that a true sportsman can pull through anything, that they have guts enough to face death in the face and defeat death."

A Final Goodbye

Jim eventually did recover from the heart attack. And, on June 2, 1945, he married a third time, to a woman named Patricia Gladys Askew. Patricia was a native of Louisville, Kentucky, and Jim had known her as a fan of his when he played professional football. Soon after they were married, the unexpected happened—Jim was accepted for duty in World War II with the merchant marines. The merchant marines are a crew of a fleet of ships that transport cargo during peaceful times and transport soldiers and weapons during wartime. Thorpe was assigned to the USS *Southwest Victory*, which carried guns and soldiers to troops stationed in India. Jim served as the ship's carpenter and loved being part of a "team" again. "We had some rough weather and some rough time," Jim said about his time aboard the *Victory*. "But we had teamwork. Cooperation is important in everything you do, and that is what made us winners."

Jim returned to a port in Jersey City, New Jersey, in September of 1945. He once again started making appearances and giving speeches—this time with his third wife by his side. Patricia was a shrewd businesswoman and negotiated more money for Jim. Under her management, he began to collect $500 per appearance.

In 1948, the Amateur Athletic Association (AAU) began organizing a Junior Olympics for teenagers. Jim thought this was a marvelous idea. "Sports will improve health and keep children out of trouble," Jim said. "If they start young, they will grow up to be healthy men and women and make a healthier nation."

In an effort to support the AAU's effort, Thorpe took a job with the Chicago Park District. He appeared across the city, promoting the Junior Olympics and teaching kids the fundamentals of track and field.

"Sports will improve health and keep children out of trouble," Jim said. "If they start young, they will grow up to be healthy men and women and make a healthier nation."

In this photo from 1948, Jim works out with kids in a Junior Olympics event for girls in Chicago.

Next, he took a job training the Israel National Soccer Team for an exhibition match against the United States, which took place September 26, 1948, in New York City. The appointment was a surprise and seemed odd to writers and fans. The president of the Israel Soccer Foundation, Haim Glovinsky, was an admirer of Thorpe's kicking ability from when he was a pro football player. "I deem it an honor to appoint America's greatest athlete to train our team," said Glovinsky. "We feel certain that Thorpe will bring our soccer team to the peak of condition for the game."

Although Israel lost the game 3–1, Thorpe, dressed in a football uniform, put on a drop-kicking display at halftime in front of the 25,000 fans at the game. From the 50-yard line, he sent three balls over the crossbar.

At 61 years old in 1948, Jim put on a fantastic drop-kicking exhibition at halftime of a soccer match between the United States and Israel.

As Jim entered his early sixties, sports observers began to fondly recall his athletic achievements. In 1950, an Associated Press poll named Thorpe the greatest football player of the half century. (Harold "Red" Grange, the player who said he'd never seen Jim in his prime, was voted second.) Later that same year, Thorpe was named the greatest male athlete of the half century by a survey of sportswriters. Thorpe received 252 votes, while the great baseball player Babe Ruth came in second with just 86. In 1951, Thorpe was inducted into the College Football Hall of Fame. Also in 1951, Jim's life story was finally made into a movie, this time called *Jim Thorpe—All-American*. A famous white actor of the day, Burt Lancaster, played the part of Thorpe. Although Thorpe had no rights over this film, he did earn $15,000 as an

In 1950, Jim was named Male Athlete of the Half Century. He's pictured here with Babe Didrikson, who was Female Athlete of the Half Century.

Burt Lancaster played Jim in the 1951 motion picture about the legendary athlete's life. The film was called *Jim Thorpe—All-American*.

advisor. The movie was received well by critics and fans alike. But in truth, it was more fiction than fact: in the movie, Jim's father was a gentle man, and Jim had no twin brother.

In 1952, Jim had surgery to remove a cancerous growth from his lips. He suffered a heart attack later that same year, but recovered. Then, on March 28, 1953, while eating dinner with his wife, Patricia, in their trailer in California, Jim had his third heart attack. He died just a short time later. He was just shy of his sixty-sixth birthday.

The famous sportswriter Red Smith wrote this of Jim after he died: "Thorpe was the greatest athlete of his time, maybe of any time in any land."

CHAPTER 12

Honor Restored

This day belongs to my dad.

—*Charlotte Thorpe*

On January 18, 1983, Jim Thorpe's gold medals were finally returned to his family at a ceremony in Los Angeles, California. It was almost seventy-one years since Thorpe had won his two gold medals in the decathlon and the pentathlon at the 1912 Olympics. It was also seventy years since he had had them taken away.

"This day belongs to my dad," Charlotte, one of Thorpe's daughters, said while standing at the podium. Each of Jim's children was given replicas of the medals. (The originals had been stolen and are still missing to this day.) And, in the record books, Thorpe's name was put in as co-champion of the two events.

Charlotte, along with other family members and historians, had spent most of her adult life campaigning to get her father's medals

Avery Brundage once was Jim's track rival, and he opposed returning Jim's gold medals, but the two men shook hands in this photo from 1952.

reinstated. But she'd met with resistance along the way—in particular from the president of the International Olympic Committee (IOC), Avery Brundage. Brundage fiercely opposed returning the medals to Thorpe. When asked about Thorpe's "crime" of playing baseball, Brundage simply answered: "Ignorance is no excuse."

Critics of Brundage, however, suspect that jealousy and **racism** were the real reasons he did not want Thorpe to have his medals back: Brundage had competed against Jim in the decathlon and pentathlon at the 1912 Games—he finished sixteenth and sixth, respectively.

Unfortunately, Brundage's successor, Lord Killanin, was just as inflexible on the return of Jim's medals. Finally, after Juan Antonio Samaranch was made president of the IOC in 1980, he restored them early in his reign. He conducted the ceremony

Jim's family celebrates with Juan Antonio Samaranch, the president of the International Olympic Committee (center), after a decision in 1983 to return Thorpe's gold medals from the 1912 Games.

on January 13, 1983, in Los Angeles, where the 1984 Olympics would eventually be held the following summer. When asked why it had taken so long for Thorpe to get back his medals, Samaranch replied, "I don't know. For the first time since I became president we studied this problem, and we solved it in two hours."

Honors Abound

In addition to the return of his Olympic medals, other honors piled on for Thorpe after he passed away. In 1963, he was elected with the first class into the Pro Football Hall of Fame in Canton, Ohio. In fact, one of the main reasons the Hall of Fame was built in Canton was because of the history of the Bulldogs' team for which Thorpe had played his first pro game. (A bronze statue of Thorpe near the entrance to the Hall of Fame is one of the first things a visitor sees.)

Shown above is a Jim Thorpe exhibit at the Pro Football Hall of Fame. Jim was a charter member of the Canton shrine in 1963.

Jim was also inducted into the National Track and Field Hall of Fame (1975), and into the U.S. Olympic Hall of Fame (1983). The following year, and again in 1998, the postal service honored the legend with his own stamp. Then, in an Internet poll conducted by ABC Sports from December 20, 2000, to January 28, 2001, Jim was voted Athlete of the Century. He received 56.7 percent of the vote—beating out the likes of Michael Jordan, Babe Ruth, and Muhammad Ali.

> . . . Jim was voted Athlete of the Century . . . beating out the likes of Michael Jordan, Babe Ruth, and Muhammad Ali.

The following November, Jim's image was put on the cover of the Wheaties® cereal box. In the photograph, Thorpe is dressed in his Carlisle football uniform and he is holding his helmet. Underneath the picture, the text simply states, "Jim Thorpe: The World's Greatest Athlete."

Why Jim Still Matters Today

Jim Thorpe died in 1953, last played in a professional football game in 1929, and made Olympic history in 1913. Yet his name, his legend, perhaps even his myth, live on every day. Why?

First, because of Jim's versatility. Try naming another athlete who has been so good at so many different things—track and field, football, baseball, even basketball—and it is all but impossible to think of someone.

Michael Jordan is probably the best basketball player ever. But he tried to play professional baseball and lasted for only one season. (He batted just .202 with a Chicago White Sox minor-league team.) Babe Ruth was a star—only in baseball. Bo Jackson excelled at both baseball and football, like Jim. But

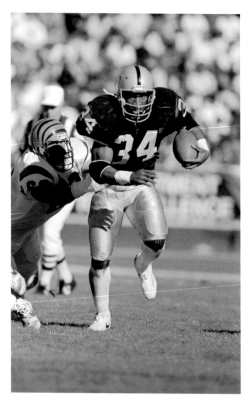

Bo Jackson, shown rushing the ball for the Raiders in this photo in 1991, was one of the few recent athletes to play two pro sports. Jackson also played major-league baseball.

Jackson played pro football for only four seasons before his body gave out—Jim was a pro for thirteen years. (Also, Bo never competed in the Olympics.)

The second reason Jim's legend lives on is his dominance over his opponents. At the 1912 Olympics, he won the decathlon with a score of 8,413 of a possible 10,000 points. The runner-up scored 7,724. Thorpe's performance would have earned him a silver medal in the 1948 Games—thirty-six years

Each year, college football's best defensive back is presented with the Jim Thorpe Award. Kansas State University's Terence Newman is shown holding the award in 2002.

later. (In comparison, sprint champions from the 1912 Games would not even have finished in the top five in 1948.)

Also factoring into Thorpe's legend is his race. He lived at a time when his people, the Native Americans, had few rights, got little respect, and were looked down upon by white people. Jim demonstrated that the color of a man's skin has nothing to do with his success on the athletic field—nor should it have anything to do with his success elsewhere.

Jim played sports at a time before big contracts, yet he never dwelled on the fact that he made little money from his incredible accomplishments. He just loved being on the field and being part of a team. "I really played for the love of the competition," he said when he announced his retirement.

Jim Thorpe, Pennsylvania

Today, Thorpe's body lies not in his native Oklahoma or in his beloved Carlisle. Oddly, he rests elsewhere in Pennsylvania.

Following Jim's death, his children thought their father should be buried back in Oklahoma, where he grew up. Fans thought he should be buried in Carlisle, where he became a star athlete. Jim's body was put in a temporary crypt, or underground chamber, in Tulsa, Oklahoma, while the family figured out a proper burial place.

Around this time, Patricia, Jim's third wife, decided she wanted to bury Jim in her own way. While in Philadelphia speaking with the NFL Commissioner, Patricia heard of two neighboring towns ninety miles north of Philadelphia that were looking to change their names and merge into one. Patricia thought the two towns could be named after her late husband.

Jim's burial site is located in Jim Thorpe, Pennsylvania. His tomb is inscribed with the sentiment that Sweden's King Gustav told Jim at the 1912 Summer Olympics: "Sir, you are the greatest athlete in the world."

Patricia drove to the towns and spoke with officials. A deal was struck. They would merge together and become Jim Thorpe, Pennsylvania. She would allow his body to be buried there. In May of 1954, the new name became official.

When visitors come to see Jim's resting place, they might be confused. But, after they read his tomb, they may stop thinking about where he rests, and instead think about the athlete Jim was in life. The inscription reads what King Gustav of Sweden said to Thorpe at the 1912 Olympics: "Sir, you are the greatest athlete in the world."

Jim was also never openly bitter about having his Olympic medals taken away from him. He endured the first real Olympic scandal, yet he soldiered on with grace and dignity. Actually, Thorpe lived through many personal tragedies. "Dad had a terrible life," said his daughter Grace. "His twin brother died when he was nine, his parents died when he was young, he lost his firstborn son. But he never lost his good spirits, he never stopped trying."

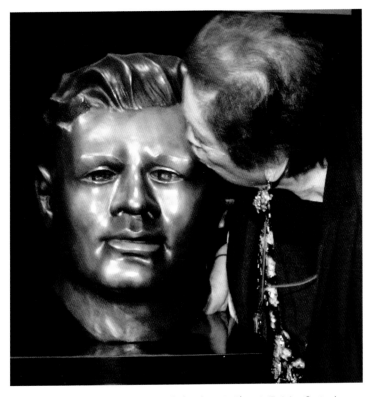

In 2000, a bust of Jim Thorpe was unveiled at the U.S. Olympic Training Center in Colorado Springs, Colorado. Jim's daughter Grace gives the likeness of her dad a kiss in this photo.

Glossary

All-America—an honor given to top amateur athletes. These athletes are usually considered the best in their position and sport and are selected by sportswriters and other voters. The athlete can be on the first-team All-America (the top), or the second or third team.

backfield—the football players on defense who are positioned behind the linemen.

batting average—a measure of a batter's performance determined by dividing the total number of base hits by the number of times at bat. It does not include walks.

broken-field running—carrying the football past the line of scrimmage and sprinting through and past several defenders.

decathlon—a track-and-field competition consisting of 10 events: 100-meter, 400-meter, and 1,500-meter runs; the 110-meter high hurdles; the discus and javelin throws; the shot put; the pole vault; the high jump; and the long jump.

D-Day—June 6, 1944. It is the day of the invasion of Western Europe by Allied forces in World War II.

double wing attack—a variant on the single wing attack. It is a running offense using misdirections.

end zone—the area at the end of the football field between the goal line and the end line.

field goals—football scores worth three points and made by kicking the ball over the crossbar and between the goalposts.

halfback—a football player who is used to run the ball as well as catch the ball on shorter passes during offensive plays.

interceptions—passes that are caught by the opposing defender, instead of the intended receiver.

novelty—something seemingly attractive just because it is new.

passing game—a play when one player throws the ball to another.

pentathlon—a track-and-field competition consisting of five events: the long jump, the javelin throw, the 200-meter dash, the discus throw, and the 1,500-meter run.

placekicker—the player who tries to make a field goal or score points after a touchdown by kicking a stationary ball.

prep school—a private school that prepares secondary students for college.

polygamy—the practice of having more than one spouse, usually more than one wife.

powwow—a Native American celebration that usually includes a feast and dancing.

punter—the football player who punts the ball, or, kicks the ball before it hits the ground.

quarterback—a football player who calls the signals and directs the offensive play of the team.

racism—a hatred or intolerance of a race other than your own.

rookie—a person who is in the first year of a sport and has little or no experience.

shutout—a defeat in a game when one team fails to score.

single wing attack—a football formation when the ball is snapped rather than handed off to the quarterback.

touchdown—the act of carrying, receiving, or gaining possession of the football across the opponent's goal line for a score of six points.

varsity—the top level of competition at a high school or college, usually referring to sports.

Bibliography

Books

Anderson, Lars. *Carlisle vs. Army: Jim Thorpe, Dwight Eisenhower, Pop Warner [and the Forgotten Story of Football's Greatest Battle].* New York: Random House, 2007.

Carroll, John Martin. *Red Grange and the Rise of Modern Football.* Champaign, Illinois: University of Illinois Press, 1999.

Crawford, Bill. *All American, The Rise and Fall of Jim Thorpe.* Hoboken, New Jersey: John Wiley & Sons, 2005.

Jenkins, Sally. *The Real All Americans: The Team That Changed a Game, a People, a Nation.* New York: Doubleday, 2007.

Newcombe, Jack. *The Best of the Athletic Boys: The White Man's Impact on Jim Thorpe.* Garden City, New York: Doubleday, 1975.

Steiger, Brad and Thorpe, Charlotte. *Thorpe's Gold: An American Tragedy and Triumph.* New York: Dell Publishing, 1984.

Updyke, Rosemary K. *Jim Thorpe, the Legend Remembered.* Gretna, Louisiana: Pelican Publishing Company, 1997.

Wallenchinsky, David and Loucky, Jaime. *The Complete Book of the Olympics: 2008 Edition.* London: Aurum Press Ltd., 2008.

Wheeler, Robert W. *Jim Thorpe: World's Greatest Athlete.* Norman, Oklahoma: University of Oklahoma Press, 1975.

Whitman, Robert L. *Jim Thorpe, Athlete of the Century: A Pictorial Biography.* Defiance, Ohio: The Hubbard Company, 2002.

Articles

Associated Press. "Jim Thorpe Has Played His Last Game; To Hunt and Fish with Indians, He Says." *New York Times*, January 15, 1926.

Buford, Kate. "Up for Auction, Thorpe's Letters Make the Past Come Alive." *New York Times*, May 30, 2007.

Daley, Arthur. "Sports of the Times: Glenn Scobey Warner." *New York Times*, September 9, 1954.

Jensen, Don. "Jim Thorpe." The Baseball Biography Project.

Lipsyte, Robert. "Backtalk; An Old Crusade Continues into the New Century." *New York Times*, January 23, 2000.

McCallum, Jack. "The Regilding of a Legend." *Sports Illustrated*, October 25, 1982.

New York Times, "'Old Jim' Thorpe Champions Tribe," December 26, 1937.

Pennington, Bill. "Jim Thorpe and a Ticket to Serendipity." *New York Times*, March 29, 2005.

Rocket, Jack. "The Great Bunion Derby." *The Running Times Magazine*.

Web Sites

"Jim Thorpe, World's Greatest Athlete, Biography." *The Official Site of Jim Thorpe*. http://www.cmgww.com/sports/thorpe/bio.htm.

National Football Foundation's College Football Hall of Fame. www.collegefootball.org.

Rodriguez, Linda. "Catching Up with the Flu: 20th Century Pandemics." *Mental Floss*, April 29, 2009. http://www.mentalfloss.com/blogs/archives/25022.

The Society for American Baseball Research. http://www.sabr.org/.

Schwartz, Larry. "More Info on Jim Thorpe." ESPN Classic, November 19, 2003. http://espn.go.com/classic/s/add_thorpe_jim.html.

Source Notes

The following citations list the sources of quoted material in this book. The first and last few words of each quotation are cited and followed by their source. Complete information on referenced sources can be found in the Bibliography.

Abbreviations:

AA—*All American, The Rise and Fall of Jim Thorpe*
BAB—*The Best of the Athletic Boys: The White Man's Impact on Jim Thorpe*
CF—collegefootball.org
CVA—*Carlisle vs. Army: Jim Thorpe, Dwight Eisenhower, Pop Warner [and the Forgotten Story of Football's Greatest Battle]*
FLU—"Catching Up with the Flu: 20th Century Pandemics"
JTAC—*Jim Thorpe, Athlete of the Century: A Pictorial Biography*
JTHP—"Jim Thorpe Has Played His Last Game; To Hunt and Fish with Indians, He Says"

JTL—*Jim Thorpe the Legend Remembered*

JTTS—"Jim Thorpe and a Ticket to Serendipity"

OCC—"Backtalk; An Old Crusade Continues into the New Century."

OJT—"'Old Jim' Thorpe Champions Tribe"

RAA—*The Real All Americans: The Team That Changed a Game, a People, a Nation*

RG—*Red Grange and the Rise of Modern Football*

RL—"The Regilding of a Legend"

SABR—Society for American Baseball Research

ST—"Sports of the Times: Glenn Scobey Warner"

TG—*Thorpe's Gold: An American Tragedy and Triumph*

UA—"Up for Auction, Thorpe's Letters Make the Past Come Alive."

WGA—*Jim Thorpe: World's Greatest Athlete*

INTRODUCTION: Simply the Best

PAGE 1 *"That was . . . my life.":* WGA, p. 99

PAGE 1 *"Sir, you are . . . world.":* WGA, p. 99

PAGE 1 *"Thanks, King.":* WGA, p. 99

PAGE 1 *"the proudest . . . [his] life.":* WGA, p. 99

CHAPTER 1: Young Jim

PAGE 2 *"Our lives . . . out of it.":* AA, p. 49

PAGE 5 *"We always had . . . house.":* AA, p. 14

PAGE 6 *"Our lives . . . out of it.":* AA, p. 49

PAGE 6 *"Our sports . . . performances.":* WGA, p. 9

PAGE 7 *"Our lives . . . reservation.":* AA, p. 19

CHAPTER 2: Welcome to Carlisle

PAGE 12 *"I believe in . . . thoroughly soaked.":* RAA, p. 67

PAGE 12 *"that young Indian":* AA, p. 165

PAGE 13 *"I have a boy . . . him Self.":* CVA, p. 103

PAGE 13 *"Son, you are . . . can do.":* CVA, p. 103

PAGE 14 *"We keep them . . . for regret.":* AA, p. 56

PAGE 15 *"Strong minds . . . not do,":* RAA, p. 102

PAGE 15 *"outstanding . . . potential,":* RAA, p. 129

CHAPTER 3: The Natural

PAGE 20 *"Nobody is . . . tackle Jim!":* RAA, p. 230

PAGE 20 *"Could I . . . try?":* CVA, p. 137

PAGE 21 *"Before Jim . . . my records.":* RAA, p. 230

PAGE 22 *"Oh, dear . . . our boys.":* RAA, p. 135

PAGE 22 *"Oh, dear . . . our boys.":* RAA, p. 135

PAGE 22 *"Nothing delighted . . . [their opponents],":* RAA, p. 197

PAGE 23 *"It was . . . the field,":* WGA, p. 55

PAGE 23 *"I want . . . football,":* WGA, p. 59

PAGE 24 *"All right . . . you'll be.":* RAA, p. 230

PAGE 24 *"Nobody is . . . tackle Jim!":* RAA, p. 230

PAGE 24 *"Jim's performance . . . to it.":* RAA, p. 231

PAGE 25 *"I consider . . . American football,":* WGA, p. 45

PAGE 25 *"The Indian boys . . . imagination,":* AA, p. 35

PAGE 25 *"When [Jim Thorpe] . . . be better.":* ST, p. 45

PAGE 27 *"I didn't . . . the bench.":* AA, p. 83

Image Credits

About the Author

Ellen Cosgrove Labrecque is a former editor at *Sports Illustrated Kids*, where she wrote about all types of sports heroes. She has also written several other sports biography books. She lives in New Jersey with her husband, Jeff (who is also a writer), and their two children, Sam and Juliet.

Index

Discover interesting personalities in the Sterling Biographies® series:

Muhammad Ali: *King of the Ring*

Marian Anderson: *A Voice Uplifted*

Neil Armstrong: *One Giant Leap for Mankind*

Alexander Graham Bell: *Giving Voice to the World*

Cleopatra: *Egypt's Last and Greatest Queen*

Christopher Columbus: *The Voyage That Changed the World*

Jacques Cousteau: *A Life Under the Sea*

Davy Crockett: *Frontier Legend*

Marie Curie: *Mother of Modern Physics*

Frederick Douglass: *Rising Up from Slavery*

Amelia Earhart: *A Life in Flight*

Thomas Edison: *The Man Who Lit Up the World*

Albert Einstein: *The Miracle Mind*

Anne Frank: *Hidden Hope*

Benjamin Franklin: *Revolutionary Inventor*

Lou Gehrig: *Iron Horse of Baseball*

Matthew Henson: *The Quest for the North Pole*

Harry Houdini: *Death-Defying Showman*

Thomas Jefferson: *Architect of Freedom*

Joan of Arc: *Heavenly Warrior*

Helen Keller: *Courage in Darkness*

John F. Kennedy: *Voice of Hope*

Martin Luther King, Jr.: *A Dream of Hope*

Lewis & Clark: *Blazing a Trail West*

Abraham Lincoln: *From Pioneer to President*

Jesse Owens: *Gold Medal Hero*

Rosa Parks: *Courageous Citizen*

Jackie Robinson: *Champion for Equality*

Eleanor Roosevelt: *A Courageous Spirit*

Franklin Delano Roosevelt: *A National Hero*

Babe Ruth: *Legendary Slugger*

Jim Thorpe: *An Athlete for the Ages*

Harriet Tubman: *Leading the Way to Freedom*

George Washington: *An American Life*

The Wright Brothers: *First in Flight*

Malcolm X: *A Revolutionary Voice*